THERE
IS NO
MESSIAH

and You're It

THERE IS NO MESSIAH

and You're It

THE STUNNING TRANSFORMATION
OF JUDAISM'S
MOST PROVOCATIVE IDEA

Rabbi Robert N. Levine, D.D.

———————◆———————

JEWISH LIGHTS Publishing
Woodstock, Vermont
www.jewishlights.com

To Judah, Ezra, and Maya:
Mom and I love who you are and are excited
about the people you may yet become.

There Is No Messiah—and You're It:
The Stunning Transformation of Judaism's Most Provocative Idea

© 2003 by Robert N. Levine

Library of Congress Cataloging-in-Publication Data
Levine, Robert N.
There is no Messiah—and you're it : the stunning transformation of Judaism's most provocative idea / Robert N. Levine.
    p. cm.
Includes bibliographical references.
ISBN 1-58023-173-X (HC)
1. Messiah—Judaism. 2. Messianic era (Judaism) 3. Redemption—Judaism.
4. Hasidism. I. Title.
BM615 .L44 2002
296.3'36—dc21

2002151090

10   9   8   7   6   5   4   3   2   1

Manufactured in the United States of America

Published by Jewish Lights Publishing
A Division of LongHill Partners, Inc.
Sunset Farm Offices, Route 4, P.O. Box 237
Woodstock, VT 05091
Tel: (802) 457-4000
Fax: (802) 457-4004
www.jewishlights.com

Contents

Acknowledgments · vii

1. What Are All You Messiahs Waiting for? · 1

2. Would Jesus Recognize the Messiah? · 15

3. Dying for the Messiah · 26

4. The Messiah Is Coming! · 36

5. We'll Survive the Messiah, Too · 49

6. Delayed Gratification · 60

7. What Should the Messiah Look Like? · 73

8. You'll Know Him after You See Him:
   Maimonides' Messiah · 82

9. Kabbalah's Call: We Are the Messiah · 89

10. The Worldwide Embrace of Sabbatai · 99

11. The Surge to Sabbatai · 111

12. A "Frank" Messianic Descent · 121

13. Hasidism: The New Look in Messianism · 128

14. The Golem · 139

15. Introducing the Universal Messiah · 148

16. Our Messianic Role · 158

Suggestions for Further Reading · 169

About Jewish Lights · 171

Acknowledgments

I WILL BE FOREVER INDEBTED to Stuart M. Matlins, the visionary publisher of Jewish Lights, for providing extraordinary guidance throughout the writing of this book. His hands-on approach made a tremendous difference in the direction and tone of the volume. Many thanks to a most talented managing editor, Emily Wichland, for her skilled and caring shepherding of this book through its growth process. Specials thanks to my editor, Michael Kress. It is rare to find an editor who is always on point and who compels you by virtue of his own insight and high quality standards to write more perceptively. Michael is that editor.

Many thanks to my literary agent, Jane Dystel, for constantly believing in me and inspiring me to flesh out those ideas as fully as I was able. She is much more than an agent. She is, and always will be, a dear friend. Her right-hand, Miriam Goderich, lent her brilliance to the thesis underlying this book.

This project would not have been possible without the tender loving care and patience of my assistant, Julie Standig. She lived with these chapters, took them home at night, helped me meet all deadlines, and was there for me to consult, worry with, and help me ultimately get to the finish line.

I am blessed with a wonderful congregation, Rodeph Sholom, whose leadership is most supportive of my rabbinical and literary endeavors. My fabulous clergy team, educators, and other senior staff inspire me with their teachings and fully share the congregational load, permitting me stolen moments for writing.

My family is central to my world. My wife, Gina, is simply the most loving, insightful, supportive mate I could ever imagine. My hectic life would not be possible without her. Our terrific children—Judah, Ezra, and Maya—teach me every day about love and responsibility. My parents, struggling with illness, sacrificed so much for me and inspire me with their example of steadfast love.

Finally, I thank God for giving us the necessary gifts and the inspiration to live a messiah's life.

◆

1

What Are All You Messiahs Waiting for?

"HEY, MISTER RABBI, who is drinking that wine?"

A braided African-American ten-year-old girl named Chaminique approached the head Seder table. Every year my congregation, Rodeph Sholom, holds what we call a Third Seder with our friends at Harlem's Memorial Baptist Church. Using a specially prepared *Haggadah,* we recount our respective bondage and liberation stories and celebrate our journeys using traditional Seder symbols, challenging text, and good music—lots of music.

Chaminique noticed a gleaming, silver Kiddush cup filled with wine. While four cups of wine were filled and drunk during the Seder experience, our Chaminique was astute enough to notice that no one even had touched that particular cup.

"We leave that cup, Chaminique, hoping that Elijah, the prophet, will come down from the heavens, visit our Seder, and drink the wine. In fact, during the Seder we open the door, hoping Elijah will arrive that very minute."

"Why do you want Elijah to come?"

"Because we believe that if Elijah comes, he will announce the coming of the messiah. You know how in your religion Jesus was sent by God to tell everyone how to live?"

"Uh-huh."

"And you believe Jesus will come again to make the world a

better place? Well, we don't believe that Jesus was the messiah, but we are still hoping that the messiah will come into our world soon."

"And you do this every year—open the door for Elijah and hope the messiah will come right after?"

"Yes."

"And you hope the messiah will make a better world?"

"Yes."

"Why are you still waiting? Why don't you do it yourself?"

THE POWER OF THE MESSIANIC IDEAL

That one was tougher than the Seder's traditional four questions. Perhaps the more important question is, "Are we still waiting for the messiah?" The answer forms the essence of this book as we come to recognize how powerful is the idea of messiah, and how long it has survived in the heart, soul, and ethos of the Jewish people. From the time our very existence was threatened in the land of Egypt, we have traveled to virtually every corner of the globe. Everywhere we went, the hope for the messiah went with us. From the smallest shtetl to the most cosmopolitan Western cities, messianic personalities attracted unbridled, uncontrollable passions and adherence. In the darkest hours of our people's collective life, the prospect of better circumstances—often involving a return to the land of Israel and rebuilding the Holy Temple—brought salve to our wounds, hope to the despairing.

But why should you and I still find the messianic ideal so engaging and so relevant? After all, we live in the wealthiest, most powerful country ever created. We Jews are the most materially blessed, politically prominent, and socially mobile community in our entire history. Why don't we simply acknowledge our blessings and congratulate ourselves for our good fortune? Why do we need to look forward to another, more hopeful time and place?

THE ATTACKS OF SEPTEMBER 11

Clearly, our complacency about life in America was shattered on September 11, 2001, when suicide bombers from Osama bin Laden's Al Qaeda network flew their planes into the north and south towers of New York's famed World Trade Center. Those immense structures crumbled, causing enormous property damage and the loss of nearly three thousand lives. In the synagogue I serve, Congregation Rodeph Sholom, on the Upper West Side of Manhattan, we lost our popular security guard, Ruben Correa (who was a firefighter by day), and three men who worked for Cantor Fitzgerald, an investment firm. They were all husbands and fathers. Brian's family is a fourth-generation member of our synagogue. Steve and his wife had just been at services the previous Saturday and were anticipating their daughter's Bat Mitzvah in the coming months. Andy was a husband and father of three small children whose youngest child, Henry, took his first steps on September 11.

These losses were devastating. Israelis live with the reality of suicide bombers every day, but never had the American continent been attacked so directly. The entire country braced for more terrorist attacks, fueled by our nation's security agencies, which issued broad, vague warnings that served to increase our sense of vulnerability and powerlessness.

APOCALYPSE NOW?

This horrific assault touched off renewed speculation about whether there was a deeper, transcendent significance to these events. Was Osama bin Laden the necessary catalyst to bring on the Apocalypse—the end of the world as we know it—and the dawn of a blessed messianic age triggered by a final, ultimate battle between the forces of good and evil? Judaism, Christianity, and Islam all have strong apocalyptic traditions, and end-of-world prophecies resonate particularly strongly among evangelical Christians today. Books on the subject fly off the shelves. Of course, there is a website (raptureready.com) and even a "Rapture Index," dubbed the "Dow Jones Industrial Average of End Time Activity" to track events that add to the communal sense of instability. According to a recent survey, seventeen percent of Americans believe the end of the world will happen in their lifetime (*Time*, July 1, 2002).

JEWISH ANGST

Few Jews fret openly about the Apocalypse, but we are similarly unnerved by September 11 and the lack of personal and group security that tragedy symbolizes. Israelis too have waged a battle against sustained and indiscriminate terrorist attacks. The vaunted military superiority of the Jewish State has been shaken by this new cruel weapon, which has made even venturing out of the house a dangerous enterprise.

Jews all over the world fear that the Palestinians want and train their children to expect not only an independent Palestinian State but the destruction of the State of Israel as well. Moreover, the recent surge in anti-Semitism, particularly across Europe, reminds Jews everywhere how thin the line is between political disagreement and personal animosity. Much to our dismay, the movement from hatred of policy to hatred of the Jewish people has been seamless.

Apparently, we have a lot to worry about. When we factor in all the other problems plaguing us, like employment difficulties, family discord, aging parents, and illness of all kinds, we Jews seem to have ample reasons for fear and pessimism.

But, should we feel this way? After all, our faith tradition assures us that we are not alone with our concerns nor without ample tools at our disposal. Doesn't the Bible give us every reason to trust that the world is in good hands? The Book of Genesis presents a God who is not an objectified being, created by some other force, but the eternal creator of every astronomical, geophysical, and biological reality we know.

God is the author of life and death, an actor in history making sure that the promise inherent in creation can be carried to fulfillment.

For our ancestors, God's power was limitless. According to the mystics, so was God's presence. In the beginning, they say, in order to make the world, God didn't have to expand divine power but instead had to contract, to reduce the divine presence, thus making room for the world.

Why would God do this? No divine press conference ever explained the motive, but God clearly wanted to do something with all that power, to make something greater than anything the world had ever seen: a human being capable of making not only his or her own mundane decisions but complex moral judgments and then acting on them. It seems, then, that God needed a partner.

The wondrous possibilities inherent in the human species were Judaism's great gift to the world. Contrast the Bible's concept of creation with the Babylonian creation myth, *Enuma Elish*, in which human beings were created to perform menial tasks for the gods, to act as bellhops to divine whims. For the Hebrew God, conversely, human beings had the power to help God save the world, to effect justice, to make weighty decisions—even to enter covenants. Each of us, then, is God's masterpiece.

GOD GIVES US REAL POWER

What a feat God performs here. In an instant God cedes omnipotence. For, by definition, if we have the power to do all of this, God simply can no longer be all-powerful.

God's extraordinary self-effacement was done for a reason. God seems to need something from us. Either God began the divine tenure as all-powerful and chose not to be, or God never was all-powerful and needed to enter into the partnership we call Covenant. Since then, God has been constantly reaching out to us. When God was about to destroy the wicked cities of Sodom and Gomorrah, God decided to tell Abraham all about it—not to provide information but to invite confrontation. Abraham's concern that the innocent might be destroyed with the wicked culminated with this ringing challenge: "Shall not the judge of all the earth in fact do justice?" This stinging challenge not only was welcomed by God but seemed to signal the passing of the divine test: Abraham was worthy to be the father of the Jewish people.

GOD NEEDS OUR HELP

Later, God seemingly could not proceed to be the liberator of the Israelite slaves in Egypt without the intercessory help of Moses. When liberated Israelites were building a golden calf at the foot of Mount Sinai, an infuriated God announced the intention to destroy the entire people. Right then and there Moses talked God out of it, arguing that God would be a laughingstock in Egypt, and that God had made a promise to Abraham, Isaac, and Jacob that they would be an eternal people. Even if the people gathered at the foot of Mount Sinai were not worthy, surely the righteousness of the patriarchs merited God's compassion now.

So, the human role in making the world better is firmly established in the Bible. But this is not enough to explain why in every generation people yearn for a messiah, a human redeemer. Why do we need outside help if the divine-human collaborative effort is so compelling? The yearning for messiah seems to represent less than a rave review for the divine commander in chief. Given the pain and persecution we have suffered throughout history, many have questioned whether God has delivered as promised. We're willing, even eager, to look elsewhere for help.

EVADING RESPONSIBILITY

But, in my judgment, the search for someone, somewhere, to come and liberate us from the present represents a cop-out on our part as well. If human beings have to take responsibility in the covenantal agreement, why are we so quick to yearn for someone to come and do what we should be doing ourselves? In arguably the Torah's most important verse, the entire community of Israel is commanded, "You shall be holy, for I, the eternal God, am holy." What an incredible gift. What power we have to rise above base, narcissistic instincts and make the world a better place.

You were not created to flee responsibility, to merely open the door for Elijah every year at the Passover Seder and think that you have done your part. In fact, you don't have to gaze longingly at the door, because the messiah is already in the room. It's someone you know well. You see, "messiah" is a translation of the Hebrew word *mashiach,* meaning "the anointed one of God." In the Bible and in later classical Jewish texts, the messiah was always quintessentially human. Many who have searched for an individual outside our purview believe that the messianic mantle must be worn by a specific person especially anointed by God for this redemptive purpose. Traditionally, there is only one *mashiach,* and we must stand by and wait for the spectacular arrival.

A NEW MESSIANIC CONCEPT

While I must acknowledge that this popular understanding has pervaded Jewish history, I still beg to differ. Thousands of years of messianic activity have produced not a single definitive inheritor of the messianic title. The Torah, our central text of faith, tells us nothing of a particular individual anointed to the exclusion of all others. In the absence of such certainty, false messiahs have emerged and will emerge, only to bring despair and disillusionment at various times in history. Even today, right-wing messianic personalities in Israel take stances that are inimical to any peace process and, in my judgment, to the time-tested Jewish values of justice and human dignity.

On the other hand, we are taught that every one of us is created in the divine image. All of us can be holy through imitating God, and the quintessential covenantal experience at Sinai established us as a "kingdom of priests and a holy nation" (Exodus 19:16).

So, you don't have to look around or look away. You don't have to wait for someone to come and do what you were put on this earth to do in the first place. Judaism empowers you, as one of God's anointed ones, to do more than you ever dreamed possible. You can even save a life, even if it's your own.

YOU ARE A POTENTIAL MESSIAH

What I am really saying is this: *There's no messiah—and you're it.*

All that some people throughout the ages believed could be accomplished only by an imported messiah sometime in the future can happen here, in your lifetime, by your use of your enormous God-given gifts. You were created with messianic potential. The following story gives you an idea of what I mean.

A member of my congregation—I'll call her Meryl—came into my study one day and announced in a certain, unabashed voice, "God saved my life last night." Naturally, I was all ears.

"You may not know this, Rabbi, but I've been a drug addict for four years. It started slowly, recreationally. I convinced myself that I was a social user, that I could stop any time I wanted. But, for a long time, I've known the truth, and I have done many things—anything—to get drugs, things that I am ashamed of. But last night I was really strung out, and I didn't care. I was at the lowest point of my life. Suicide looked really good to me. I had all the pills laid out and opened a bottle of vodka. I was going to finish it off—and me as well.

"But, just then, the doorbell rang. You have to understand, Rabbi, I have alienated all my friends. I have abused them, pushed them away, stolen from them, even. But the doorbell rang last night and it was Elaine, my best friend from college. I hadn't seen her in over a year. She told me last night that a strange feeling had come over her, a feeling so strong she couldn't ignore it. She lives an hour and a half away, Rabbi. But she got in her car and drove here as fast as she could to ring my doorbell at just the right moment.

"No one is going to convince me that this was an accident, just woman's intuition or a premonition. God spoke to her last night and saved my life."

As I have said, the word "messiah" identifies one chosen by God for a special reason. Elaine was the messiah that night. She responded to the call and saved a life. So can you. You may not get the kind of premonition Elaine did. You may not know for sure when and how God may want to work through you to accomplish the otherwise unaccomplishable. There simply may come a time when you get a sign, a feeling, a searing recognition that there is something you can and must do for yourself, for someone else, for your community, for God, or for all of them simultaneously.

Think about it—a hundred people could have walked by the biblical burning bush and said, "Wow, that's a strange bundle of sticks. How weird," and walked away. Only Moses saw the presence of God in that same bush.

Moses was chosen, anointed by God, for a mission. So are we. We are created with the ability to respond to God's messianic call. If ever we sense an irresistible impulse burning within us to do something we didn't know we wanted to do or are capable of doing, that very well may be God's call to us: not to wait for someone else to arrive but to be God's partner on earth.

The Bible presents some incredible models of just those kinds of people for us to follow. In Egypt, when Moses was still a babe in swaddling clothes, two midwives, Shifra and Puah, found the courage to defy Pharaoh's orders to put all first-born Hebrew males to death. Moses' sister, Miriam, a Hebrew girl, seeing Pharaoh's daughter pick Moses out of the bulrushes, found the courage to run to her and ask if this member of the royal family needed a nursemaid—who, unknown to Pharaoh's daughter, would be Moses' own mother. In turn, this daughter risked a lot by bringing a Hebrew child into the palace of the father who had ordered the genocide of such children.

Later, Moses ventured out to see the suffering of his people. Seeing an Egyptian overlord brutally beating a Hebrew slave, he looked side to side, saw no one there, and took justice into his own hands. Based on this verse, the later rabbinic text *Pirke Avot* teaches, "In a place where there is no one else, try to be a *mentsch*" (my translation).

It's a lofty, heady role for us, but the Bible knows it's not such a cushy job being God's anointed one. So, you won't be shocked to know that people weren't lining up to seek the job as God's anointed. In fact, in the biblical period, no one went around calling themselves *mashiach*. That was the term David used to describe the first king of Israel, Saul, but Saul never used it for himself. Having seen Saul's tragic downfall, David would claim the title of messiah only at the end of his life, in a song of thanksgiving that praised God for showing abundant kindness to "his anointed one and his seed now and forever more" (2 Samuel 22:51). Never did he claim the title during his days as military warrior or political ruler. It was an identity he felt much more comfortable adopting at the end of his life, looking back from a safe distance. After all, it's not easy being the messiah!

There was yet another reason why this was not a role to be envied. As I mentioned earlier, the messianic era, particularly in our early history, was believed to be preceded by a climactic battle between the forces of good and evil. Apocalypse precedes the dawn, and such anticipated devastation sends shudders down the spines of even the most skeptical of our people. In all the turmoil the messiah is no meek bystander. His role will be to "smite the earth with the rod of his mouth and with the breath of his lips shall he slay the wicked" (Isaiah 11:4).

In these various apocalyptic messianic images, the world as we know it disappears and is replaced by a new reality. While the anticipation of God's triumph over the forces of evil and the return of the dispersed exiles to the Promised Land surely would bring some comfort, there could be no assurance that those who listened to the prophet's vision would survive the onslaught preceding the ultimate reward. You should not be surprised to read later in this book that most Jewish messianic visions either downplay or eliminate altogether any apocalyptic precondition for ultimate redemption.

Times, eras, even preconditions change, but the messiah idea survived as a vivid prospect for the people of Israel. But, as I will demonstrate in this book, messianism is a constantly evolving concept. What changes is far more fundamental than the identity of any single messianic personality. We will see the sands shift on some crucial questions: Need we only to sit back and wait for the messiah, or be proactive in the advent? What will the world look like when the messiah does come? Will the *y'mot Ha Mashiach*, the days of the messiah, embody a particularistic vision of our people returning from exile to the Promised Land, or will they reflect a more universalized or more personal vision? Finally, are we to yearn for a specific individual to help deliver us, or can we play a significant role in the transformation of the world from a mess to the messianic?

IDENTITY OF PERSONAL MESSIAH

My own understanding in this matter is clear. I share Jewish tradition's belief in a personal messiah, but not in its understanding that there is only one legitimate candidate. For a people who across the spectrum barely recognizes one another as Jews, how could we ever reach consensus on a messianic candidate? Such a miracle will have to await the Coming of the Messiah! Nevertheless, we still can anticipate a time when people will live up to their potential as Jews and as people. As we pray, study, and fulfill *mitzvot,* we will be inspired to live Jewish values and thus, hopefully, will treat all persons with respect and bring to fruition the repair and redemption of our world.

MESSIAH IS HERE

This can't happen without the *mashiach,* who, thankfully, already has arrived and is living closer to us than you ever could have imagined. There's no messiah—and you're it!

You are crucial to this effort, and your work will not be easy. You will be unpopular for refusing to settle for the status quo. You may drive yourself crazy by expecting higher standards of conduct from yourself, and then from others, than you ever dreamed possible. You may even doubt whether or not you're doing the right thing, since so many other people seem to be doing things differently. But just remember that your life here on earth is no accident. Your life is a special gift, a sacred gift. You are here for a purpose, and it's important to get in touch with that blessed fact.

SPECIAL GIFTS

And if you think it's hard being the messiah, try ignoring the call to be the messiah. Jill Kornfeld found that out for sure. As part of her nursing school training, Jill had an opportunity to experience work life on many floors in the hospital. She spent an unforgettable two weeks on the pediatric cancer floor. Even when she was off duty, she couldn't get the faces of those kids out of her mind. She lay in bed and visualized each child—faces swollen and hair lost from drug therapy—their eyes exuding a sad wisdom learned from their long, bitter, heroic struggle.

Jill knew that if she went to work in pediatric oncology, she would live on an emotional roller coaster. She was not sure she was up to it and kept trying to find ways of avoiding the assignment. But something inside of her kept drawing her back there. So, when she graduated from nursing school, she found herself in "peds" battling cancer with her kids.

It didn't take long for parents to discover the special gifts she possessed. Her smile brought cheer to dour lives. Jill seemed to know just what to say to each kid in every situation. Even when she drew blood, which was a constant task on that floor, she had a way of distracting the kids so they barely noticed the sharp needle protruding from the skin.

One day a parent came to her. She and her daughter were leaving the hospital after a particularly grueling chemo cycle.

"One time my daughter was throwing up all night. She told me she had had it. She didn't want to fight anymore. She was ready to throw in the towel. My husband and I didn't know what to say any more. Then you, her nurse, walked in. I don't know what you said or did, but the next thing I knew my daughter was up combing her hair, looking in the mirror, thinking about the coming week."

Tears were streaming down her face. "Jill," she said, "I don't know how to thank you. You are an absolute gift from God."

You can be too. I believe we were sent here to be God's eyes and ears, heart and soul, helpmates in the ongoing struggle against things we cannot understand but must nevertheless overcome.

WHAT ARE YOU WAITING FOR?

God anointed every one of us. You don't have to wring your hands and bemoan your fate. You don't have to look at life's events and wonder why God is doing this to us. That question presupposes that we have nothing to say about human history and presumes no personal responsibility for our destiny. In my judgment, you must not sit passively and wait for the coming of a redeemer to save us in our hour of need.

The responsibility to repair the world is ours. As *Pirke Avot* emphasizes, "You are not required to finish the work, but neither are you free to desist from it."

Chaminique asked the key question at the Passover Seder: "Why are you still waiting? Why don't you do it yourself?"

So, what are all you messiahs waiting for?

———————◆———————

2

Would Jesus Recognize the Messiah?

F OR THOUSANDS OF YEARS, people of many faiths have been searching for the messiah. This quest for someone outside of ourselves and our surroundings to save us from our current plight tells us as much about our lack of self-confidence and our trust in institutions and their leaders as it does about the condition of the world. So, we look out there, anywhere, for someone, anyone, to do what we should do for ourselves.

Almost everybody wants the messiah to come. Almost no one knows when and how the messiah will arrive and what impact the phenomenon would have in our lives. But we fervently keep yearning for anyone and falling for anything.

The following paid announcement placed by a sidewalk evangelist was published on the sports page of the *New York Times:*

EIGHT COMPELLING REASONS WHY CHRIST IS COMING VERY SOON!

HOW TO BE PREPARED FOR HISTORY'S GREATEST EVENT.

The reasons given in this ad, combed from no fewer than one hundred and sixty-seven supposed "converging clues," range from the seemingly positive (Israel's rebirth) to the much more negative (plummeting morality and increase in earthquakes) to the totally bizarre (the increased centralization of world financial and political power in the hands of the "Antichrist").

The ad brooks no doubt, entertains no hedge. Christ, the acknowledged messiah by believing Christians, is returning to earth very soon, and we had best prepare. "We receive him by faith. We receive him by personal invitation." The ad even provides the exact prayer to say if you want to ensure the blessed coming.

Those who announce the second coming with certainty surely share these maddening traits: they know exactly who the messiah is, when the messiah is coming, and what we can do to bring it on. Some evangelists actually welcome war, earthquakes, and other forms of upheaval because they herald the coming of the Apocalypse and the appearance of the Antichrist, all of which herald the second coming of Christ.

RELUCTANT MESSIAHS

Sorry to put the brakes on the pending arrival, but identifying, packaging, and delivering the messiah, the anointed one of God, has never been accomplished so easily. First of all, the best candidates for messiah never shared this unbridled enthusiasm. As we have noted, King David resisted the title until the very end of his life. What the prophets shared in common was total resistance to their mission because they knew they would spend their lives telling people who didn't like them what they didn't want to hear: failure to live up to the covenant would result in severe punishment.

So, the anointed one of God often didn't know himself who he was until it was too late, didn't want the job, and was not happily received when he did reluctantly assume the mantle. How did the one man most often recognized in the role, Jesus of Nazareth, fit into the picture? Did he break the mold and happily embrace the messiah role, or should we assume that he fit it rather well and was a typically reluctant messianic candidate?

WHO WAS THE REAL JESUS?

That's a great question. Unfortunately, no one will be able to answer it with any certainty. There was no eyewitness evidence for exactly who Jesus was, what he said, what he claimed for himself, and what he expected others to do with his words. The Gospels of Matthew, Mark, Luke, and John, which speak of Jesus' life, were written at least a full generation after his death and can in no sense be called either objective history or biography. They were written with the express purpose of inspiring Jews to accept Jesus, this itinerant teacher from the Galilee, as that generation's messiah, the anointed one of God.

Because Jesus was a Jew, because his message was aimed largely at Jews, and because he is the most recognized messianic candidate in history, thus becoming the template against which all future messianic candidates must be measured, it is necessary in my judgment to include Jesus in a study of Jewish messianism. In fact, the end of the first century C.E. was an ideal time for an impassioned advocate like Saul of Tarsus to make a legend out of this bright, spellbinding interpreter of the soul and essence of Judaism. Saul, who became Paul after a stirring roadside revelation, got a great message and messenger to work with and one invaluable thing more: opportunity. Ancient Israel, now named Palestine, was seething with anger and humiliation. Situated at the heart of major trade and transportation routes, Palestine had always been in play, subject to the empire-building lusts of one superpower, then another.

The startlingly successful revolt of Mattathias and his sons, the Maccabee brothers, against the Syrian Greeks, beginning in 165 B.C.E., had given the Jews a fleeting sense that they could hold destiny in their own hands and create an independent Jewish theocratic state with God as ultimate ruler. The emerging Roman Empire, which usually cared about little except collecting taxes from its subjects and keeping the peace, quickly dashed the Jews' hopes for even spiritual autonomy by making it clear that no Roman subject could worship anyone but Caesar. To underscore this order, they placed a Roman eagle over the Temple door, resulting in the predictable fury of the Jewish populace.

THE POLITICAL ESTABLISHMENT IN JESUS' DAY

No Jew could harbor the illusion of Rome as benevolent dictator any more. The Romans were out to crush the Hebrew religion and the Jewish spirit. Everyone was united in that common understanding. Where they differed was in what to do about their situation. The political establishment formed two main groups: the Sadducees and the Pharisees. The Sadducees, mostly descendants of Judah Maccabee's clan, called the Hasmoneans, were members of the priestly class, in control both of the Temple and the powerful Sanhedrin. They had much to gain from mollifying Rome by keeping the peace, thereby maintaining their prerogatives of power. The much-maligned Pharisees, though they despised Roman encroachment, believed that Jewish life was not tied to any one time or place. They were also willing to enter into negotiations with Rome, confident that the Jewish future didn't depend on maintaining the Temple as the nerve center of Jewish life. Pharisaic doctrines, which included belief in life after death and resurrection, gave the Jews transcendent weapons to deal with the painful facts on the ground. But in their own way, the more adaptable Pharisees relied on the status quo just as the more aristocratic Sadducees did. Their numbers and influence were growing—so, really, what could be so terrible?

Other groups were far less hospitable to Rome's far-flung designs. The Zealots, an ultranationalistic group, were determined not only to resist political and spiritual assaults with the sword but to wage civil war against those Jews who, in their judgment, were not sufficiently militant. Believe it or not, these Zealots burned Jewish food rations from inside the Temple compound, ensuring that fellow Jews had no choice but to fight to the death. The last of the Zealots reportedly committed suicide on top of Masada rather than subject themselves to Roman rule.

Then there were those who opted out of the rough and tumble. The Essenes were a group of ascetics who authored the Dead Sea Scrolls, discovered in the twentieth century in the caves of Qumran. They guarded their identity and privacy carefully, revealing their practices only in the writings they left behind. The Essenes appeared to live simply, far from the explosive population centers of Palestine. They were true fundamentalists, hewing to the strictest interpretation of the written law, and not looking for the compromise necessary to live comfortably amidst other peoples and cultures.

Each of these groups believed that they not only were dealing with Rome in the best way possible but were doing so according to God's will. They were responding to the commanding voice of God as interpreted through the authority of Torah. All believed that they and they alone possessed God's revelatory wisdom. They and they alone possessed the Truth and would act on it, even if it killed them.

So, where does Jesus fit into this picture? Great effort has been expended to determine how to align him properly. Was he a Pharisee? A Sadducee? An Essene? To fully associate Jesus with one political party or another would be to do what Jesus never did and would be to instantly know more about him than we actually do know or ever will know. We never will learn whether Jesus identified himself with any of these groups. Surely, his spiritual odyssey would have found some common ground with both the Pharisees and the Essenes. But he very much worked outside the system and surely would not have publicly affiliated with any party. Most likely he felt he was more effective staying outside of the political establishment, seeking to be regarded as an authentic Jew, well able to determine God's word and zealously desirous of spreading God's truth as far and wide as he possibly could.

IT'S A MATTER OF SPIRIT, NOT POLITICS

Jesus did respond—not politically but spiritually. All evidence points to the fact that Jesus put himself squarely in the prophetic tradition. The very beginning of the Gospel according to Mark, the oldest and closest chronologically to the life of Jesus, makes this connection in the very earliest verses:

> The beginning of the good news of Jesus Christ, the son of God. As it is written in the prophet Isaiah: "See I am sending my messenger ahead of you, who will prepare your way; the voice of one calling out in the wilderness; prepare the way of the Lord, make his path straight." The kingdom of God has come near; repent, and believe in the good news (Mark 1:1–3, 15).

The prophet speaks not because he wants to but because he must. The message is that the world God has envisioned is within our grasp, but the people must travel a distance in order to meet God in this covenantal effort. What behavior is more crucial than repentance? The Jewish High Holy Days are built around the human capacity and need for such transforming behavior.

But if Mark presents the authentic voice of Jesus here, he clearly is a very different kind of prophet. The message of the Hebrew prophets is harsh and condemnatory, obliged to spell out the consequences that will befall the people because of their sinful behavior. True, God will never abandon them, and God's kingdom eventually will be established. But there will be much pain before the gain.

JESUS' MESSAGE IS APOCALYPSE-LITE

Jesus' message, quite to the contrary, is entirely upbeat. No punishment, no exile are in the offing. There may be a few apocalyptic elements in Jesus' presentation, but it is clearly apocalypse-lite. No determinative battles between forces of good and evil are contemplated, no wanton death and destruction. The kingdom of God is being gently established on earth by God's grace with relatively little demand upon God's constituents.

What Jesus does seem to want is for Jews to prepare for the time when God's kingdom will be established on earth. What is required is not an abandoning of the essence of Judaism—Torah and ritual remain essential—but an embrace of the implications of these teachings as he sees them.

THE KINGDOM OF GOD IS AT HAND

The Sermon on the Mount makes this clear:

> Do not imagine I've come to abolish the Torah or the prophets; I've come not to abolish but to complete. I tell you solemnly, until heaven and earth disappear, not one jot or tittle will disappear from the Torah—not until everything has come to be (Matthew 5:17–18).

The Ten Commandments, for example, constitute a fine guide for normative society. But the goal of life, for Jesus, is to prepare for the ultimate time of morality and justice. So, *Thou shall not murder* no longer suffices. Even anger against your fellow is no longer tolerated. *Thou shall not commit adultery* isn't a high enough standard in this kingdom. Now you cannot even countenance lust in your heart. *Eye for an eye, tooth for a tooth* will not be either desirable or necessary any more. In God's kingdom, violent impulses will be defeated by turning the other cheek. *Love your neighbor* will be replaced by *Love your enemy,* and the two will be indistinguishable. In other words, Jesus seems to be saying, live how you would live in the kingdom of heaven and you will play a role in bringing it on (Matthew 5:38–44).

It is not hard to understand Jesus' appeal, particularly to the weary underclass of society. Though some doubtless were drawn to his seeming ability to perform miracles trumpeted by his followers, surely the first-century world in which he lived was full of such "performers." Many more people doubtless were drawn to his message. In a world in which one superpower, then another, held Palestine in a suffocating choke hold, Jesus offered the people something they could do with their frustration to usher in an entirely new kingdom. If his message seemed self-righteous, ascetic, even off the mark from what they knew to be normative Judaism—well, maybe that was what God intended in the first place. Maybe this prophet understood what is implicit in Torah better than anyone else.

HARD TO FIND HISTORIC JESUS

The historic Jesus must have been a most interesting and appealing, if controversial, teacher. But this Jesus is close to impossible ever to discover. Neither the gospels nor the letters of Paul are, or purport to be, objective history. Neither, for that matter, is the Hebrew Bible (or Old Testament, as later Christians came to call it). The Hebrew Bible describes the evolving covenantal relationship between God and the people rooted in their land. Torah celebrates God's providential power while underscoring the human responsibility inherent in this ancient covenant.

The New Testament is designed to launch a new relationship between God and people, based around the concept of the crucified and risen Christ figure. Every effort is made to lure Jews and others to this new understanding and to elude state repression in the process. So it is understandable why Jews would be cast in the least appealing light in the pages of the New Testament, and Roman authorities would be seen as sympathetic rulers trying to navigate between intractable foes.

Understand that crucifixion was nowhere to be found in the Jewish lexicon of behavior but was an everyday punishment for the Romans. As famed scholar Morton Scott Enslin has noted, "The Roman law was clear: persons who cause sedition or upheaval or incite the mobs are, depending upon their civic status, libel to crucifixion, or to be thrown to the wild beasts, or to be banished to an island" (*The Prophet from Nazareth,* p. 182).

But in the gospels, the Roman governor Pontius Pilate magnanimously declares that Jesus is innocent and washes his hands of the whole affair: "I am innocent of the blood of this righteous man; see to it" (Matthew 27:24).

JESUS AND THE JEWS

He clearly protested too much. Jesus' blood certainly was on Pilate's hands and on his hands alone. But it is probable that Jewish authorities were anxious to get Jesus off the streets. That his teachings might incite the growing crowds to engage in unruly, even revolutionary, behavior was only part of the problem. If even a portion of what the gospels report is true, Jesus' behavior in the Temple, overturning the tables of the money-changers and encouraging mob behavior, was so dangerous to the peace that the Jewish authorities felt that they had no choice but to stop him.

Their concerns were not only for social order but also for their own political survival. They were acutely aware that if they did not keep social and political order, the Romans would come rolling in with an iron fist and would eviscerate the Jewish community and their way of life in a brutal show of force, including the all-too-common use of crucifixion as capital punishment.

But who was this man? Or, more to the point, what did he claim for himself? Central to our inquiry, did he regard himself as the messiah or not? No doubt he felt singled out by God for his singular prophetic mission, so that the words he spoke did not feel like his any longer, but God's. He was compelled to speak. That he may have called himself "Son of Man" may have been a public posturing of humility, consistent with the Psalmist who calls out to God,

"What is man that Thou art mindful of him? And the Son of Man
that Thou even thinks of him?" (Psalm 8:4).

Surely, some were already prepared to make loftier claims
about Jesus' identity even in his lifetime. Some Jews, though a dis-
tinct minority, were even prepared to identify him as the long-
awaited anointed one of God.

DID JESUS THINK HE WAS THE MESSIAH?

When Peter and others call him the messiah, the anointed one
of God, he very well may have blushed. When the High Priest
asked him directly if he was the messiah, Jesus would say only,
"You have said so" (Matthew 26:63–64). But he might have been
secretly delighted. As I said before, King David was one of the few
to ever call himself messiah, so Jesus was in lofty company. Even
so, it is highly doubtful that Jesus himself expected to make a
speedy, supernatural, postcrucifixion return as a divine being
incarnate, such that he was an actual part of God in human form.

Saul of Tarsus' mission was to make of Jesus' life a pretext for
the return. He led us to think that what happens in this world is
of relatively little consequence. Everything we do is preparation
for a new world order, the dawning of the kingdom of heaven.
This thorough downgrading of the value of life on earth was a
radical departure from normative Judaism. This surely was Paul's
dream. This surely was not Jesus' dream.

As Jesus made his way toward Jerusalem he might have begun
to slowly believe that he and his message were one. But for him,
the messianic age, so close at hand, would take place here on
earth, to be effected by human beings, altering their behavior to
live passively and righteously in the kingdom of heaven, which
could happen in real time and in this world.

It is quite possible that toward the end of his tragically short-
ened life, Jesus warmed considerably to the label "messiah," just

as King David did, and used such a status to urge upon his followers strictly ascetic, life-changing behavior. But there is nothing in the historical record to suggest that he believed that the messiah would come to earth as a result of apocalyptic violence or return in a Second Coming. Probably, he would have been content if more Jews, whose respect and love he craved, simply would have acknowledged the first Coming and had embraced the messenger together with his message.

3

Dying for the Messiah

S OME JEWS, desperate to embrace a messianic figure, accepted Jesus as God's anointed one. A small group of them followed Paul into the nascent faith of Christianity. The remainder stayed within the fold, believing there was no contradiction between remaining Jewish and accepting Jesus. The vast majority of Jews neither embraced Christianity nor became "Jewish-Christians." They couldn't accept Jesus, mainly because they didn't see the positive ramifications of the messiah's arrival here on earth. If the messiah in fact had come, why hadn't the oppression of the people eased at all?

So, the wait continued—and it was excruciating. Religious leaders were under intense pressure to help their people against the onslaught of Roman oppression and humiliation.

The most prominent of these leaders was the greatest Jewish figure of the first century C.E., Rabbi Akiba, who, after becoming a Torah scholar later in life, developed a wide following because of his immense learning, brilliant teaching skills, and ability to inspire his followers.

But now, a generation after Jesus had lived and died, Rabbi Akiba was in turmoil. Few scholars had penetrated the depths of Torah as he had, but the Truth he demanded from the text still eluded him. God's way is justice, but the world reeked of cruelty. And if God is ever-present, how could the pagan Roman Empire topple God's people and destroy the Holy Temple, God's sacred residence on earth?

Akiba could not fathom the thought of God's abandonment. On the contrary, he was convinced that God was waiting for people and in fact had singled out messiahs, anointed human beings, who could achieve divine goals. Surely God had designated a redeemer who could now lead the people to victory over the cruel oppressor.

Akiba was desperate to discover who the messiah was. He would leave no stone unturned until he found the messiah's identity. Together with three other sages, a desperate Akiba entered what the Talmud calls the *Pardes,* a mysterious realm commonly understood to mean the world of mystical speculation. But a prominent scholar believes that, shockingly, Akiba was actually looking for the messiah in the newly born faith called Christianity, which was coming to prominence under the persistent work of Paul of Tarsus.

Professor Samson H. Levey argues that the *Pardes* Akiba entered is the Hebraized form of the Greek *Paradosis*, the term used by Christians to designate the early teachings of the Church. Certainly, Akiba did not emerge as a convert to Christianity, but his willingness to go there shows how desperate he was to find a way out of Israel's tragic fate (*Judaism*, Fall 1992, p. 334).

It appears that Akiba's extraordinary act of messianic search did not go unpunished. Johanan ben Nurri, a second-century rabbi, gave surprising testimony in a midrash:

> I call upon heaven and earth to testify for me that on more than four or five occasions I had Akiba publicly flogged, because I had brought accusations against him before the patriarch Rabban Gamaliel (*Sifre, Kedoshim* 4:9).

Though the sin committed by Akiba is not stated in this midrash, surely a sage of Akiba's stature would not have been flogged for a violation of ritual law or even a political infringement. Nothing less than flirtation with doctrines totally at odds with the Jewish faith could have produced such a sanction.

Failing to find the answer there and feeling shame for his dalliance in another religion, Akiba emerged as a scathing critic, engaging in polemics against heresy in general and Christian "heresy" in particular. In a famous passage in the Talmud, Akiba declared, "All Israel has a share in the world to come." He then proceeded to enumerate those who had no share in the world to come and pointedly included those who read the *hizonim,* the books excluded from the Hebrew canon, chief among them those of early Christianity.

AKIBA'S FIERY MESSIANISM

In his demeanor, Akiba displayed the quality of a zealot, veering sharply from one polemic to the next, so desperate to find Truth he was willing to act before fully considering the consequences, convinced that what he did was correct even if he was soon convinced otherwise. So, he set off with equally ferocious passion in precisely opposite directions, sure of the righteousness of his position, unwilling to listen to any reason beyond his own, brooking no nuance or compromise.

The presence of Rome on Jewish soil was so odious for Akiba that he likely had gone even where Jews dare not go to seek redress. Though he repented for that journey, he could no longer return unrepentant to the Jewish establishment. The humiliation of his punishment must have kept him at a distance, breeding resentment from those who still sought accommodation with the Roman oppressors even after they had destroyed the Temple and humiliated our leadership.

AKIBA EMBRACES BAR KOKHBA

Akiba felt increasingly desperate, impassioned, alone. Advancing years made him ever more determined to help his people avoid further catastrophe while he still could. Perhaps this explains his embrace of a relatively obscure and hot-tempered military leader named Simeon ben Koziba, known as Bar Kokhba ("son of a star"), as the messiah. He based this designation on his interpretation of a biblical verse: "A star has marched forth out of Jacob" (Numbers 24:17). Akiba believed that verse to be a sure prediction of Bar Kokhba, the son of a star, as messiah. In fact, when Rabbi Akiba saw Bar Kokhba, he would say, "There he is, the king, the messiah" (Jerusalem Talmud, *Taanit* 4:68d).

Why Bar Kokhba? It's hard to know for sure. There are few historical or rabbinical sources about him, and those that exist are hardly flattering. In demonstrating his physical prowess, the Midrash said he would catch catapulted stones and throw them back into the crowd, often killing several people. This lack of judgment pales next to his initiation rite for his men: he asked them to cut off one of their fingers as a sign of loyalty (*Lev Rabbah* 2:56). Bar Kokhba also had a terrible temper and once killed his own uncle, the great Rabbi Eleazar of Modiin, for not being instantly responsive to his words.

So it's hard to understand how Akiba could support such a person. Even more puzzling is Bar Kokhba's seemingly utter disregard for God's power. The story is told that when he and his soldiers were going out to war, rabbinic leaders assured them that God would be there to help them. "He will not assist nor weaken," retorted Bar Kokhba (Jerusalem Talmud, *Taanit* 4:68d).

One rabbinic tale had Bar Kokhba going even further.

> And when he went out to war against the Romans, his heart grew proud and called out, "Oh Lord, God of Hosts, do not stand at our right hand, nor be against us, for You, Oh God, have abandoned us. We, ourselves, shall be victorious over the enemy" (*The Aggadah Treasury* 1:192).

How, then, could Rabbi Akiba embrace him so passionately? In his important work *The Bar Kokhba Syndrome*, Professor Yehoshua Harkabi, a professor of International Relations and

Middle Eastern Studies at Hebrew University in Jerusalem, cites several possible reasons. First, old age had impaired his judgment. According to the midrash, Akiba was a shepherd for forty years, studied for forty years, and led Israel for forty years. Time was catching up to him. He may have been close to eighty years old when the Bar Kokhba rebellion began.

AFFLICTIONS OF LOVE

A second reason is that his own theology caused him to downplay the effect defeat would have on his people. Suffering, for Akiba, was not a consequence of God's wrath but of God's love. These "afflictions of love" caused the individual to become introspective and to examine why suffering occurred, since it had to be happening for a reason and for his own good.

It is fair to assume that a man of such wisdom and stature believed that Bar Kokhba represented the best hope to finally throw off the Roman yoke. Although Akiba may not have loved everything about Bar Kokhba, and out of desperation may simply have wanted to back the "winning horse," we shall see in a moment that no objective analyst of the situation could have come to that conclusion. Whatever the reason, Akiba's backing in the third major battle against Rome in a one-hundred-year period clearly gave Bar Kokhba credibility. And he did have his notable military successes, particularly in conquering Jerusalem. Roman casualties were so heavy in that theater of war, in fact, that Emperor Hadrian was unable to inform the Roman Senate of victory with the usual formula "I and the legions are in health."

The destruction of Roman legions was an impressive feat, but it hardly constituted the beginning of a lasting victory over Rome. In fact, Bar Kokhba couldn't seem to convince the northern Galilean Jews to join in the battle; this failure surely contributed to a lack of military momentum.

These northern Jews were fortunate to escape the carnage. By the time the Romans were through, the results were calamitous for the Jews. The Roman historian Dio Cassius' description is chilling:

> Only a few of them were saved . . . nine hundred eighty-five villages lay in ruin. In the raids and battles, five hundred eighty thousand were killed. When we count the number of those who perished in famine, plague and fire, it is clear Judea became a complete desolation (Dio Cassius, *Roman History*, LXIX, 14:1–2).

BAR KOKHBA'S FAILURE

Even if these figures are a bit exaggerated, the number of people who suffered death, slavery, and displacement was enormous. Historian Michael Avi-Yonah estimated the Jewish population in the country as 1.3 million before the Bar Kokhba rebellion but only seven to eight hundred thousand after the three-and-a-half year rebellion. Jerusalem, too, lay in ruins. The Romans destroyed just about every settlement in Judea. What remained were small, isolated communities on the fringes of the country. The name "Judea" was even changed to the "Syrian Province of Palestine" (*In the Days of Rome and Byzantium*, p. 25).

Shockingly, the Rabbis of the Talmud had relatively little to say about the Bar Kokhba rebellion. However, they did offer this one devastating comment:

> For seven years the gentile inhabitants, who had settled in the land after Judea was emptied of its Jews, harvested their vineyard without manure as fertilizer, but, rather, with Jewish blood . . . they killed until the blood flowed out of the doorways . . . , until the horses waded in blood up to their nostrils and the blood moved stones the size of forty seas and flowed into the sea for a distance of forty miles (*Lamentations Rabbah* 2:79).

This was arguably the greatest catastrophe to befall the Jewish people until the Holocaust in the twentieth century. How could it have happened? How is it possible that Bar Kokhba—or Akiba, for that matter—could have so miscalculated the military abilities of the two foes? It is possible that the cumulative hatred of the Romans was so strong that any additional provocation would push the Jews to react in a nonrational way, totally divorced from rational military calculations. That spark, explains Dio Cassius, was readily apparent:

> At Jerusalem the Emperor Hadrian founded a city in the place of the one which had been razed to the ground, naming it Aelia Capitolina; on the site of the Jewish Temple of the God of Israel he raised a new temple to Jupiter. This brought on a war of no small importance nor brief duration, for the Jews deemed it intolerable that foreign races should be settled in their city and foreign religious rites instituted there (Dio Cassius, *Roman History*, LXIX, 12:1–2).

Turning Jerusalem into the pagan city of Aelia Capitolina was more than a humiliation for the Jews of Palestine. The Rabbis taught that there were only three calamities for which Jews were expected to give their lives: murder, incest, and idolatry. It is easy to see how some in the Jewish populace felt that they had no choice but to rise up against this overwhelming provocation. More than self-respect was at stake. Their understanding of the fundamental relationship established in the covenant between God and the Jewish people demanded an immediate and offensive response. Hadrian's apparent banning of castration, which included provisions against circumcision, was further evidence that the Romans expected more than just lifestyle changes. They demanded the end of the Jewish religion.

So the Jews did not lack for sufficient provocation. As first evidence of their intentions, following the Bar Kokhba rebellion, Hadrian totally outlawed the practice of Judaism and the study of Torah throughout the land. According to the Talmud, Akiba himself was tortured to death for failing to heed this ban.

CHOOSE LIFE OVER NOBILITY

Given Rome's totalitarian stance, perhaps the demand to lay down our lives for sacred principle should be viewed as a noble response. There are those who would have argued so then, and certainly some who feel that way today. But surely, few could possibly countenance the destruction of the Jewish people even to protest such Roman humiliation. What good is principle with no Jews left to defend it?

It is doubtful that the thousands of people who went to war behind Bar Kokhba were committing mass suicide. This was no Masada writ large. But no sober military calculation alone should have led to the conclusion that the Jews of second-century Palestine were ready for the battle against Rome and the sustained war that would follow. The Bible commands us to choose life and treats each moment of life as sacred. Surely there are other ways to resist even idolatrous challenges, short of the risk of mass self-destruction.

There was only one way that Bar Kokhba could have rallied as much of the country as he did to such an ill-fated war: the conviction that this was the climactic messianic battle to restore not only political sovereignty but the promised kingdom of David in the Promised Land. Rome provided the tinder, Akiba the cover, for the people to embrace this man who was on a brave but clearly misguided mission.

We see the results when people who are desperate to find a messianic solution to their plight follow a destructive force and take other people with them. In our own era, Osama bin Laden believed he was God's anointed one, attacking the "satanic empires" including America and Israel. A key feature of his Al Qaeda terrorist network and the Arab terrorist groups linked to Iraq, Iran, Saudi Arabia, and Yasser Arafat is their ability to recruit suicide bombers to do such things as fly into the World Trade Center and walk into Zion Square in Jerusalem and blow themselves up and everyone who is tragically in their path. They succeed because these attackers believe they will be rewarded in Paradise for their actions and that they are helping to create a more just world here on earth.

Like all messianic aspirants, these protagonists will be judged by whether or not their actions produce anything but bloodshed and a renewed cycle of violence, so devastating to human beings on both sides of the conflict as well as to the cause they purport to champion.

Some have drawn an analogy between Bar Kokhba and groups like the Stern Gang, who used militant tactics to defeat the British and the Arabs at the time of the establishment of the State of Israel in 1948. It is still possible to debate the morality and effectiveness of their tactics, but these were hardly "messianic" activities. They were secular, political responses—fervent attempts to fulfill the Zionist goals of reclaiming the land of Israel—and those groups never claimed to be doing their work as God's anointed ones. Therefore, they could engage in furious debate with Prime Minister Ben Gurion and his Haganah defense forces over tactics that would actually work rather than debate over divine truth.

Messianic personalities always believe they are unconditionally right, even when the facts on the ground seem to contradict them. That is why the terrorists of our day, like Bar Kokhba, are dangerous. Perhaps that is ultimately what separates them from successful revolutionaries such as the Maccabees, who revolted against the Syrians and Greeks. Though such terrorists believe their cause is just, their miscalculation as to what means are necessary to achieve their ends have proved in the past to be much too costly for the Jewish people. Embracing a war that never would have been fought save for its messianic implications, Bar Kokhba, Akiba, and their followers caused a tragic loss of life, political identity, homeland, and self-esteem for the Jewish people. It would be nice to think that we have learned permanent lessons from this debacle, but this would be far from the last time when large numbers of people would give up their lives to follow a false messiah.

BAR KOKHBA SYNDROME

Professor Harkaby labels this behavior the Bar Kokhba Syndrome and defines it as a display of rebelliousness and heroism totally detached from responsibility for the consequences of one's actions. Subsequent Jewish history tells the tale of many who have suffered from this very ailment.

Probably the first victim of the Bar Kokhba Syndrome was Bar Kokhba himself. Perhaps he didn't display responsibility in leadership because he was too delusional to do so. In his mind he didn't need God's help. In his mind, he didn't really need anyone, nor did he consider the consequences for others.

Thus, it is possible and necessary, in my judgment, to reject Bar Kokhba but to embrace an activist posture in an effort to change the world. Narcissism or fame ought not to be the motivation. Our goal should be to help improve the lot of others in line with God's covenantal expectations that we are to be concerned with justice and human dignity. Messianic pursuits should be altruistic and socially centered, not self-centered.

Bar Kokhba had the messiah complex, and he was the one and only candidate for a messiah in his day and perhaps the only beneficiary. The hundreds of thousands who backed the wrong candidate paid for their zeal with their lives—countless thousands of lives. Yet, the appetite for finding the messiah was still not quenched. Lacking confidence in God and surely in themselves, the Jewish people, exiled from their land, persisted in looking elsewhere, anywhere, for a messiah to save them from external persecution and inner torment.

◆

4

The Messiah Is Coming!

THE SOLDIERS IN Bar Kokhba's messianic army had internalized
Bar Kokhba's zeal and seemed to have little inclination to
question the rationality of what they were about to do. They
would not listen to the worrying concerns of their wives, or anyone else for that matter. The hero within each of them had been
awakened, and he would not resist a chance to alter the course
of history with his own two hands.

As you might expect, there were voices of caution and dissent.
Rabbi Johanan ben Torta reacted sharply to Akiba's endorsement
of this insurgent: "Akiba, grass will grow from your cheeks, and
the son of David will not yet have come" (*Lamentations Rabbah*
2:54). But no one was listening as thousands rushed headlong to
do the manly thing.

Now, devastation ruled the land. Not only did people have to
mourn death and destruction on a massive scale, not only were
they faced with religious persecution that made even the study
of Torah punishable by death, but they had to do so with the
humiliating knowledge that they had followed a false messiah. It
is one thing to sacrifice all you hold dear for a sacred principle
for which you would be prepared to give your life. But for a self-
absorbed militant with delusions of grandeur?

What could those soldiers do with their anger and humiliation? They were too exhausted and scattered to lash out against
their oppressors or leaders. So many people were leaving the land

of Israel that the Rabbis had to employ both the carrot and the stick to prevent migration. It is a *mitzvah* to live in Israel, they implored in teachings like this one: "Let a man dwell in the land of Israel, even in a town inhabited mainly by gentiles, rather than outside the Land, even in a town entirely inhabited by Israelites" (*Tosefta Avodah Zorah* 5:3). Dwelling in the land of Israel was, to these sages, as meritorious as the observance of all the precepts of Torah.

Other sages were not so gentle. Rabbi Simeon said, "So long as the Israelites are on the Land, it is as though the Land was not conquered. If they are not on the Land, it is as though the Land were conquered. . .whoever leaves the Land in peace time and goes abroad, he is accounted as an idolater" (*Baba Batra* 91 a–b). Rabbi Simeon ben Eleazar widened the attack by saying that Israelites who live outside the Land are idolaters (Mehilta de R. Ishmael, *Massechta de Ba-hodesh VI*, p. 227).

STILL IN SEARCH OF THE MESSIAH

Their words did have some effect on many people. But you would think that following the Bar Kokhba debacle, Jews of all ideological stripes, wherever they lived, would reject the very notion of messiah, horrified by what they had witnessed and deathly afraid of suffering another jolt of crushing disappointment when messianic hopes inevitably were dashed. But that's not what happened. If anything, messianic speculation increased. Surely God would not bring us to this Land just to have us absorb so crushing a blow. Surely there is a greater plan for redemption. If Bar Kokhba was the wrong agent for deliverance, many people were still determined to find out who the true redeemer mght be.

This was a remarkable response to calamity. Survey four thousand years of Jewish history, through repeated attempts to crush, expel, isolate, and exterminate the Jewish people, and you will discover similarly remarkable resilience in our people. We simply refuse to be defeated. Triumphant hopefulness is captured in Israel's national anthem, *Hatikvah,* which contains the words, *Od lo avdah tikvatenu,* "We have still not lost our hope, the two-thousand-year-old hope to be a free people in our own land, in the Land of Zion and in Jerusalem."

It was that hope that sustained Abraham on his journey to a new land and faith.

It was that hope that sustained Moses and Miriam in the desert.

Hope does not usually result from a sober calculation of odds. It comes from the romantic stirrings of the heart. As the noted modern Orthodox scholar Professor David Hartman puts it, "Hope is a category of transcendence which enables man not to permit what he senses and experiences to be the sole criterion of what is possible" (*Joy and Responsibility,* p. 232).

EMBODYING HOPE

The prophet Jeremiah embodies this quality in a remarkable scene in Chapter 32 of the Book of Jeremiah. The southern kingdom of Judah was under siege by the enemy from the north, and the embattled king of Judah, Zedekiah, imprisoned Jeremiah for his prophecy that Judah would be defeated—not because a superior power would win a military victory, but because God would punish the people of Israel for their gross abrogation of their covenantal responsibilities. In the prophet's view, the Babylonian king, Nebuchadnezzar, was God's agent in carrying out this retribution.

So, Zedekiah refused to accept this shocking message as God's word and jailed Jeremiah for sedition, knowing that Jerusalem, the capital city, and the entire kingdom of Judah was about to fall. Jeremiah, from his jail cell, inspired hope in his people with a deceptively simple act: he bought real estate from his cousin. Actually, he exercised the inheritance right of redemption for family land that was about to be sold because of economic hardship.

Jeremiah undertook a careful transaction according to the law, actually paying for the land in the presence of witnesses, properly recording the deed, and burying evidence of the purchase in an earthen jar—all in front of the Jews who sat in the court of the prison.

He did this to underscore God's message that though they were being punished for their transgressions, including idolatry, their homes, fields, and vineyards would be possessed by them again in the Land. God would bring them back from the countries to which God had exiled them in anger, and they would rebuild their Land. "And they shall be my people, and I will be their God. . . . And I will make an everlasting covenant with them" (Jeremiah 32:38–40).

Jeremiah's contemporaries had few objective reasons to harbor hope in the face of impending destruction. But the prophet's everlasting gift is the hope of a better world that we can help to create.

CAN'T LIVE WITHOUT HOPE

It is that hope that sustained the late Rabbi Hugo Gryn even in a concentration camp. In 1944, the German army had moved into his hometown of Berehovo, in what was then Czechoslovakia, and deported his family to Auschwitz. There his father took precious margarine rations and hardened them to make Chanukah candles.

"Papa," his son said to him, "you need these to eat; you must keep your strength; you must stay alive."

"My son," he replied, "our experience here has taught us that you can live two weeks without food, two days without water. You can't live two minutes without hope."

As a rabbi I have witnessed remarkable displays of courage fueled by hope. A mother whose son died of a brain tumor said to me that the only reason she could go on after suffering such a tragedy was that her son had taught her the absolute value of life. "He just wouldn't quit. He always believed that there would be a tomorrow."

HOPE EVEN IN DESPAIR

Recently I participated in one of the most moving Bat Mitzvah ceremonies of my life. Peter was in the hospital dying of cancer. His wife, Sally, called me to come over. He was slipping fast. They were both hoping that he would live until Emily's Bat Mitzvah, some months away, but it was not to be. I went to the Holy Ark, cradled a Torah in my arms, and rushed to the hospital. At 7:30 that evening, I conducted Emily's Bat Mitzvah service. Peter, Sally, their son Teddy, and Emily sang the prayers. Then, wrapped in a tallit, Emily's parents said the Torah blessings. Peter looked at Emily's tear-stained face and told her how wonderful she was, how proud he was of her. It was his deathbed blessing: his expression of confidence in her, the transfer of undying love and resolve from parent to child. During his illness Peter never gave up the fight. He battled to the very last moment. We felt his strength that night. We felt his blessing. He died at midnight.

Such determination never to give in has always characterized our people. Josephus, the most prolific historian for the period of Rome's destruction of Israel, wrote that even years before the destruction of the Temple, prophets and seers who envisioned the Temple in ruins spoke at the same time in the most glowing terms about a new Temple descending from heaven. When the sages Rabbi Johanan ben Zakkai and Rabbi Joshua saw the Temple in flames, Joshua exclaimed, "Woe unto us that this place, where the inequities of Israel were expiated, lies in ruin." Johanan steadfastly replied, "My son, be not grieved. We have a means of atonement that is its equal, namely the practice of loving deeds" (*Avot de R. Nathan* version II 7:11a).

In every era, Jews have not let adversity dash their dreams. They have just found alternate means to achieve the same ends. Clearly the messiah was not embodied in the person of Bar Kokhba. In the people's minds, however, the messenger was wrong, but not the message. The messiah is coming. It was left to talmudic sages to speculate as to when and how the messiah, in fact, will come. And they did not disappoint.

CALCULATING THE COMING OF MESSIAH

The dates and times of the messiah's coming have been subject to continual speculation. A *Tanna* (a second-century Rabbi of the early Talmud period) of the School of Elijah taught: "The world will exist for six thousand years. For two thousand years there'll be desolation; for two thousand years, Torah; and for two thousand years there will be the Days of Messiah" (Talmud, *Sanhedrin* 97a). Among the Rabbis were many "calculators of the End," as they often were called, who were believed to possess revelations directly from Elijah. Thus it is related that Elijah said to Rav Judah, "The world shall endure no less than eighty-five jubilees, and the Son of David shall come in the last jubilee."

Said Judah to him, "At the beginning of the jubilee or at the end?"

"I know not."

"Shall it be completed or not?"

"I know not" (*Sanhedrin* 97b).

Another text has Elijah speaking to Rav Judah, the brother of Rav Salla the Pious: "You say, 'Why doesn't the messiah come?' Today is the Day of Atonement, yet there were many virgins violated in Nehardea" (Talmud, *Yoma* 19b).

It is hard to know whether the Rabbis' tongues were firmly in their cheeks. Did they really take seriously the attempt to find the due date for the messiah?

PRECONDITIONS FOR MESSIAH

The sheer volume of messianic speculation points to an affirmative answer. Believe it or not, competition among the Rabbis proliferated as they tried to predict not only when the messiah would come but the preconditions of the messiah's arrival. Here is a sample of this speculation:

> The Son of David will not come until a fish is sought for an invalid and cannot be procured.
>
> The Son of David will not come until even the most powerful kingdom ceases to hold power over Israel.
>
> The Son of David will not come until there are no conceited men in Israel.
>
> The Son of David will not come until all justices and officers are gone from Israel. •
>
> "When you see a generation ever dwindling, hope for the messiah. When you see a generation overwhelmed by many troubles, await him."
>
> Rabbi Johanan also said, "The Son of David will come only in the generation that is either altogether righteous or altogether wicked" (Talmud, *Sanhedrin* 98a).

What these sources do not clarify is what, if anything, we have to do to make it all happen. There was a great debate about this in the Talmud between two great sages, Rav and Shmuel. "All the appointed times of redemption are over, and the messiah depends wholly upon repentance and good deeds," declared Rav, clearly on one end of the spectrum. In response, Shmuel stated, "It is sufficient for the mourner to remain in his mourning" (*Sanhedrin* 97b). Suffering alone warranted the messiah's coming for Shmuel, whereas concrete moral action was demanded by Rav. When asked by his disciples what a man should do to save himself from the throes of the messiah, Rabbi Eleazar responded, "Let him occupy himself with the study of Torah and with good deeds" (*Sanhedrin* 97b–98a). But Maimonides resolutely saw no cause and effect between human conduct and the coming of the messiah. Redemption occurs by divine decree, he taught, so repentance is not a precondition but the grateful, human response to the miracle of messiah (*Joy and Responsibility,* p. 237).

WE MUST NOT SIMPLY WAIT FOR MESSIAH

In the key debate about whether you have to act or simply wait to bring on the messiah, I firmly side with those who reject passivity. This clearly is the Torah's position, as we learn in that dramatic moment at the Sea of Reeds. With raging waters in front of the Israelites and the Egyptian army in pursuit from the rear, Moses cried out to his desperate people, "Do not be afraid. Stand by and witness the salvation of God. God will fight for you, and you may hold your peace."

Incredibly, God rejected such an approach: "Why are you crying out to me? Speak to the children of Israel and tell them to go forward."

God didn't create us to simply sit back and wait for life to happen. God didn't establish a covenant with us so we would become silent or passive partners.

Judaism's teaching here, its strong emphasis, is clear. Ultimately it's not what you feel that counts; it's not even what you believe. You are what you do. And you don't have to wait for anyone else.

You can restore self-worth to those who think they are worthless.

You can break the chains of bondage.

You can feed those hungry for food or human contact.

You can pray for people who are sick, then go and visit them.

You can save a life. Maybe your own.

HOW TO SUSTAIN HOPE

While interred in a concentration camp, renowned psychoanalyst Viktor Frankl described what sustained his hopes on the brink of despair:

> There were shouted commands: "Detachment, forward march! Left-2-3-4! Left-2-3-4! . . . Caps off!". . . . Occasionally I looked at the sky, where the stars were fading and the pink light of the morning was beginning to spread behind a dark bank of clouds. But my mind clung to my wife's image, imagining it with an uncanny acuteness. I heard her answering me, saw her smile, her frank and encouraging look. Real or not, her look was then more luminous than the sun which was beginning to rise.
>
> A thought transfixed me: for the first time in my life I saw the truth as it is set into song by so many poets, proclaimed as the final wisdom by so many thinkers. The truth—that love is the ultimate and the highest goal to which man can aspire. Then I grasped the meaning of the greatest secret that human poetry and human thought and belief have to impart: *The salvation of man is through love and in love.* I understood how a man who has nothing left in the world still may know bliss, be it only for a brief moment, in the contemplation of his beloved. In a position of utter desolation, when man cannot express himself in positive action, when his only achievement may consist in enduring his sufferings in the right way—an honorable way—in such a position man can, through loving contemplation of the image he carries of his beloved, achieve fulfillment . . . .
>
> I did not know whether my wife was alive, and I had no means of finding out (during all my prison life there was not outgoing or incoming mail); but at that moment it ceased to matter. There was no need for me to know; nothing could touch the strength of my love, my thoughts, and the image of my beloved. . . . "Set me like a seal upon thy heart, love is as strong as death" (*Man's Search for Meaning,* pp. 56–58).

We saw that same sentiment on September 11, 2001, when some husbands phoned their wives (that was usually the case) from the top of the World Trade Center, knowing that they were in imminent danger but wanting to profess their love. Sometimes they could only reach an answering machine, and there they recorded their last loving messages.

As I mentioned earlier, the congregation I serve, Rodeph Sholom in Manhattan, lost three members who worked for Cantor Fitzgerald on the 104th floor of Tower One; our nighttime security guard, who was a firefighter by day; and a number of friends and relatives. A cousin of one of our members told me that she was talking to her husband, who was in the second of the Trade Center towers when one of the airplanes exploded into Tower One, where their son was working. Neither husband nor son survived, but she will never forget her husband's final, endearing words. Though those words were private—the last loving communication between husband and wife—it is not hard to imagine their power as she keeps them with her the rest of her life.

The human ability to connect so powerfully to another, our ability to feel real concern for another human being and to know that someone in turn cares for us, can keep us afloat when the waters are rough and muddy, and it can sustain us in our memory bank for a lifetime.

POWER OF PERSONAL CONNECTION

The legendary Jackie Robinson found this out when he was first called up to the Brooklyn Dodgers. The year was 1948. The Dodgers were playing the Reds in Cincinnati, Ohio. The color barrier was being broken, but the fans filled the stadium with the most vile of taunts and curses. Jackie Robinson stood isolated, protected from neither fan nor teammate.

Then something extraordinary happened. The Dodgers' shortstop, Peewee Reese, who had grown up in the nearby southern city of Louisville, simply walked across the diamond, paused, and placed his arm around the shoulder of his teammate. Suddenly a hush descended over the crowd. Clearly, they were mesmerized at the sight of two baseball players standing next to each other with a white arm draped over a black one. Clearly, Jackie Robinson and those who made his entrance into baseball possible did an incredible amount to break down the barriers of prejudice and ridicule that were commonplace in our country. That one act of human decency buoyed the hopes of many black Americans that some day they would find common cause with whites and help fulfill the promise of this great "Land of the Free."

It's the power of personal connection. Perhaps the greatest source of hope is the connection we have felt with God for thousands of years. Biblical Jacob found God alone in the dark of night. Jacob had deceived his brother and fled for his life. Asleep, he dreamed of angels ascending and descending from the heavens. He awoke and declared, "Surely God is in this place and I did not know it" (Genesis 28:16). That faith sustained him during a twenty-year exile from his family.

Moses found God only when he went out to see the suffering of his people. The injustice and degradation he witnessed overwhelmed him. He felt an overpowering urge to right this wrong, so he slew the Egyptian overlord.

Moses didn't hear voices from the heavens. He felt an overpowering urge to do justice from within the recesses of his mind and heart.

God works most effectively from inside of us.

HOW WE FIND GOD

When I wrote my first book, *Where Are You When I Need You? Befriending God When Life Hurts,* I was sent on a speaking tour. Everywhere I went in this country I asked this question: "Have you had a personal experience with God?" The response was overwhelmingly positive. I was not surprised.

But when I asked under what circumstance these experiences had occurred, I was not fully prepared for the answer. The majority of respondents said that they found God not in joy but in sorrow. When they had suffered personal tragedy and despair, it was then that they felt God's presence. Perhaps this is the true meaning of Psalm 23: "Yea, though I walk in the Valley of the Shadow of Death, I will fear no evil, for Thou art with me." It is there that God is felt most intensely. It is in that vulnerable state that we can best let another in. A wonderful Chasidic expression captures this truth: There is no room for God in people who are too full of themselves.

We make room for God more in emptiness than in excess, when we can feel strength that is not inherently ours. There is a force inside insulating us from totally losing it, from sinking into despair—a force that helps us keep going and that eventually leads us from darkness to light.

This is God. And we are God's agents for good, covenantal partners in the struggle for human dignity and justice, in the constant quest to create a better world. We are coconspirators in bringing hope to the world.

So we don't have to wonder whether the messiah will come. The messiah will.

You don't have to calculate when the messiah will come. The messiah already has.

You don't have to wonder who the messiah is. *You* are.

DIAMONDS IN THE ROUGH

Rabbi Bernie King tells the story of Rabbi Shlomo Carlbach speaking to members of Manhattan's Diamond Dealers Club. He was challenged by one of the attendees as to why he wasted so much time with lowlifes and crazies. Reb Shlomo responded by asking the group whether they had ever accidentally thrown out a million-dollar diamond in the rough. "Never!" shouted the group, "An expert would know the worth of that which he held in his hand."

"I'll let you in on a secret, my friends," Reb Shlomo responded softly. "I'm also an expert on diamonds. I walk the streets every day, and all I see are the most precious diamonds walking past me. Some of them you have to pick up from the gutter and polish a bit. But once you do, oh how they shine! So you see, the most important thing you have to know in life is that everyone, everyone, is a diamond in the rough" (Sermon printed in *American Rabbi*, Spring 1998, pp. 4–5).

You have the power to make your world glitter a little more every day.

———————◆———————

5

We'll Survive the Messiah, Too

ONE DAY I WAS SITTING in one of those massive traffic jams we've all experienced. It was so bad that people were getting out of their cars and speculating about what was going on. Was it an accident? Construction? An elderly man shook his head. "It ain't either of those things. It's the Connecticut lottery. It's up to eighty million dollars. That's where we are all going. You know what they say, 'All it takes is a dollar and a dream.' Well, I got me two hundred dollars 'cause I got me some big dreams."

Playing the lottery, it seems to me, is a lot like hoping for the messiah. It's the big bang, the instant jolt that will change your life. The chances of its happening are slim, but there's always that little hope. As yet other lottery slogans put it, "You can't win if you don't play." "You have to be in it to win it." So, as we have seen, many did plunge into messianic activity, even going so far as to fight battles to the death, seen as necessary precursors to the messianic era.

YOU HAVE TO PLANT THE TREE

But not everyone was so caught up in the fervor. A famous rabbinic dictum warns, "If you are in the middle of planting a tree and word comes that the messiah has arrived, finish planting the tree, then go seek the messiah" (*Avot* de R. Nathan XXI: 33b–34a).

Not only does this comment denote justified cynicism about the coming of the messiah, it also teaches something profound about Judaism. It's not enough just to have faith, or to pray, or even to live in Israel. You have to act. You have to plant a tree that will take root and grow, not only for your benefit but for all the generations that will come after you.

That's the meaning behind the talmudic story of a sojourner who saw Honi, the Circle maker, now an old man, planting a tree.

"Hey," shouted the stranger, "how long will it take for that tree to grow?"

"About seventy years," comes the reply.

"And you think you'll live to see the fruits of your labor?" scoffed the stranger.

"Well, my grandparents planted for their children, my parents planted for us, so I'll do so for all the children who are to follow," replied Honi (Talmud, *Taanit* 23a).

In this regard, it seems there is a profound difference between Eastern and Western religions. Hinduism and Buddhism concern themselves with the endless cycle of life and death, focusing on reincarnation and persistent attempts to be released from the endless cycle of death and rebirth. The goal of all this is *nirvana*, the pleasure felt in breaking this circular whirlwind. A life, then, seems to be just one more stopping place on this perpetual journey.

YOU ARE WHAT YOU DO

In Judaism, every life has supreme value. God takes note of each one of us. In the High Holy Day liturgy, God is pictured recording all of our deeds, because every one ultimately matters. So, in the Jewish life cycle we celebrate the birth of every child, joining together to celebrate the brit or baby naming, and welcoming that child into the covenant between God and the people of Israel.

Bar and Bat Mitzvah is unique among all the religious faiths in singling out thirteen-year-olds and teaching impressionable teenagers that they're crucially needed to build a Jewish future and build a better world. In turn, they have real responsibilities to other people. Life is not only about the *I* but is quintessentially about the *we*. Bar and Bat Mitzvah powerfully teaches this truth: What is most important is not how you feel, what you believe, or what you promise. In Judaism, you are what you do.

BRING LIGHT WHERE THERE IS DARKNESS

So, you can't just sit back and enjoy your life. You have to bring light to those who sit in darkness. That's why, when asked what she was going to do after winning a major prize in the lottery, a nurse named Yolanda said she was going back to the hospital the very next day.

"But you never have to work another day in your life," shouted a reporter.

"Honey, I gotta work. That's what God put me here on this earth to do. Besides, my patients need me."

There are people who need you. Life presents these opportunities to you every day. Don't squander them. Figure out the reason you were put on this earth, and fulfill that potential. To wait for the messiah is to squander the chance to do something worthwhile with the gift of life. Don't wait for someone else to make something out of your life. Do it yourself.

Rabbi Laura Geller, the first woman to be the spiritual leader of a major Reform congregation, tells the story of a woman passing by a sign in a bookstore in Berkeley, California. In great big letters, it read:

PRAYER DOESN'T WORK.

That caught her attention, so she went closer. Underneath, in smaller letters, it read:

MEDITATION DOESN'T WORK

then in smaller letters still,

KABBALAH DOESN'T WORK

underneath that,

PSYCHIATRY DOESN'T WORK

At the very bottom of the sign were these words:

NONE OF IT WORKS
YOU HAVE TO WORK

SWITCHING TO THE ACTIVE MODE

When you switch from the passive to the active mode, you will appreciate how awesome the world really is. That may seem ironic, because you might think that if you kick back and idle your motor, you'll appreciate your surroundings more. But it seems to be that the person who works hard all day appreciates the fruits of labor more than someone who is handed everything on a silver platter. Those who live with a sense of entitlement rarely wonder why they are so fortunate. They may ask, "Why me?" when their self-important worldview is shattered by the painful reality that intrudes into every life. They never ask, "Why me?" when they are endowed with blessing.

DON'T TAKE LIFE FOR GRANTED

Rabbi Harold Schulweis shares the perspective he gained as a patient in a coronary care unit:

> Miracles—not in mountains moving or seas splitting, or people walking on the surface of waters—but in the rapture of breathing and sighing, in understanding a word spoken or a paragraph read, in following an argument, in recognizing a face, in waking to the ecstasy of ordinariness, the extraordinary ordinariness.
>
> Consider the heart, the soul of life. One half pound, the size of a closed fist. . . . This heart, now wounded, scarred, occluded, atrophied, is deliberately stilled, the patient anaesthetized, marsupialized, heparinized, intubated, cannulated. The patient prepared, subject to hypothermia, cardioplegia, oxygen pumped to allow skillful courageous hands to sever sternum bone and muscle, to penetrate the heart itself so that it can be given life.
>
> Who now dares take life for granted? Who can yawn in the face of this. . .worldly resurrection? Whose tongue can remain locked, whose lips sealed before such awesome wonder? (*Moment,* November 1981, p. 46).

As the sages put it, either everything is a miracle or nothing is a miracle. People often ask me why there were so many miracles in biblical times—the bush that Moses saw that would not be consumed, or the splitting of the Sea of Reeds. My answer is that there are the same number of miracles happening today. You just have to open your eyes. The poet Elizabeth Barrett Browning captures this sentiment in her famed poem "Aurora Leigh":

> Earth's crammed with heaven;
> And every common bush afire with God;
> But only he who sees, takes off his shoes,
> The rest sit around and pluck blackberries.

In our prayer book we thank God every day for the "miracles" of everyday life. But I don't want you to respond to miracles by taking off your shoes. For you are not just what you experience. You are what you do.

MESSIANIC WORK IS NOT PASSIVE

While many resisted messianic temptations because they saw the consequences of following a false demagogue, others wanted to live authentic Jewish lives that did not depend on waiting for someone else to help them fulfill their potential. Prayer, repentance, and good deeds avert the severe decree, we are taught on the High Holy Days, and many people want to follow that prescription for living, which is so anathema to messianic passivity.

All real life is meeting, taught the philosopher Martin Buber. That's what makes us truly human. I always thought, Buber wrote, that at the end of my life I would die with a book in my hand. Now I know, at the end of my life, I want to die with another human hand in mine.

We are most alive when seeking relationships. Your heart never beats quite so fast as the moment before you see your blind date. We want to connect, to love, to care, to need and be needed. When those relationships suffer, we ache mightily.

We are alive to love and loss, hope and despair, pain and joy. We are alive when we are in motion, not when we wait for something to happen.

FEARING APOCALYPSE

Besides fear of activism on behalf of false messiahs or passivity in anticipation of the next one, there may be yet another reason why many people didn't yearn for the messiah. The biblical prophets taught that the messiah would not just arrive one day before the dawning of this new era. They would have to endure the dreaded

Apocalypse: dramatic, determinative, and destructive battles between the forces of good and evil. The prophet Ezekiel depicted the final battle as between God and the mythic figure Gog from the country of Magog (Ezekiel 38–39). In later rabbinic literature, Magog became personified as Gog's partner. The war of Gog and Magog is viewed as the great Armageddon preceding the messianic era.

The biblical Book of Daniel is considered the only fully apocalyptic book to make it into the Hebrew Bible. As is characteristic of apocalyptic literature, the Book of Daniel is careful to disguise the identity of the nations that are to be destroyed in the process, portraying them as mythological beasts, half lion or ram or goat. Always present is an angel to interpret these omens of destruction and to predict the saving of Israel on or before that climactic Day of the Lord.

But who wants to live through the Apocalypse—particularly since it is hard to tell an apocalyptic battle from a plain old John Wayne shoot-'em-up? And the person leading you through the decimation before the dawn could very well be another messianic pretender.

So, you understand why many found it wise to take a rain check on Apocalypse. If that's what you have to endure to experience the messiah, we can live without it. Probably a whole lot longer without it.

Perhaps now we can better understand the wisdom in the story of the Jew who came home from the synagogue and excitedly told his wife, "Guess what I heard, dear? The messiah is coming any day and will take us all to the land of Israel."

His wife became hysterical. "Chaim, it took us years to be able to afford to move into this neighborhood and buy the house we've always wanted. Now, we spent a fortune fixing it up. We don't want the messiah's coming to take all this away from us."

"Okay, okay, don't worry," responded the harried spouse. "We survived Pharaoh; we survived Haman. With God's help we'll survive the messiah too!"

NO PRECONDITION FOR THE MESSIAH

The famed philosopher Maimonides argued against those who believed that the Apocalypse was a necessary precondition for the messiah: "At that time there will be neither famine nor war. . . the one preoccupation of the whole world will be to know the Lord. Let no one think that in the days of the messiah any of the laws of nature would be set aside . . . the world will follow its normal course. The words of Isaiah, 'And the wolf shall dwell with the lamb, and the leopard shall lie down with the kid' (Isaiah 11:6) are to be understood figuratively, meaning that all Israel will live securely among the wicked of the heathens who are likened to wolves and leopards." As the Talmud teaches, "The sole difference between the present and the messianic days is deliverance from the servitude to foreign powers" (*Sanhedrin* 91b) [*Hilchot melachim,* Chapters 11 and 12].

In Maimonides' view, the challenge of being human is not upended in the messianic era. As Dr. David Hartman put it, "For Maimonides, the open-endedness of human choices will remain even during the messianic age. His vision of hope incorporates uncertainty; the human condition is not transcended, and moral struggle remains an abiding feature of history" (*Joy and Responsibility,* p. 236).

MESSIANISM IS THE REALIZATION OF SINAI

Messianism, to Maimonides, is the full realization of the Sinaitic covenant. We lose neither the freedom of choice nor the "instinct for evil." Again in Hartman's words, "Messianism, then, is not the end of ordinary human history, but is a description of political and social conditions where the demands of Sinai are fully realizable" (Ibid, p. 244).

But do we really need the messiah or the messianic era to fulfill the promise of Sinai? In Judaism, the most important event that has happened to us as a people is not the Holocaust, as tragic as that historical event was, but our redemption from Egyptian slavery and our standing at Sinai to receive the Torah. These experiences didn't happen only to our ancestors. In our faith they happened to us.

Every Passover, we carefully set the table with materials that arouse the senses of taste, smell, and sight, because we somehow need to transport ourselves back there. We have to inhale degradation, to somehow know what it is like to feel the sting of the oppressor's whip, to rejoice as the shackles come off and the journey begins, to embody the hopefulness about the future as we open the door to Elijah and the potential for full human redemption. As the *Haggadah* itself reminds us, "In every generation, a person should feel as if he or she was personally taken out of slavery in Egypt."

AS MESSIAH, YOU CAN REPAIR THE WORLD

We were there. And because we were there to accept the covenant, we can live it ourselves in community with others. Here and now. Without an outside messiah. As the well-known author Leonard Fein put it in a memorable talk at my congregation in 1992: "Judaism is a living culture and commitment, or it is a vestigial curiosity. However sweet the folklore, however evocative the nostalgia, it is not the essence. The essence, the specific genius of the Jew, is the proposition that the world is not working the way it was meant to, that it is a broken, fractured world, and that we are implicated in its repair. . .we were taught and now we teach that in order to live a productive life, partnership in the act of creation is required. . . . Judaism is not a shawl we put on or take off as occasion seems to warrant. . .Judaism, properly understood, is a way of life. . .so it is not the services we attend but the services we perform that define us."

So, the world is a broken place. What are you going to do about it?

RESPONDING TO BROKENNESS

A story is told about a bird that was caught by an old cat. The cat gnawed at the bird and held it with its paws for a while but didn't really hurt it. Then the cat simply lost interest and went on its way. Stung, the bird rose to its feet and tested its wings. There was no damage, but the bird just didn't fly. A farmer witnessing the event commented, "The bird is still caught in its brokenness." Many people are similarly caught, but we can help release them. So, again, I ask: what are you going to do about it?

We are the people who have smashed the idols, eaten the bread of affliction, and broken the chains of bondage for ourselves and for others. We are the people who have said no to death and yes to life, who have believed that not only will there be a tomorrow but that tomorrow can be better than today. We have done that too *without* the messiah.

WE ARE WHAT WE DO

Another tale is told about a group of Jews who came to the Gates of Heaven only to be told by the caretakers that while they deserved to enter heaven, they'd have to wait while their living quarters were being prepared. In the meantime, they'd have to take up residence down below, in hell. But a week later, the devil put in an urgent call to the caretaker in heaven and pleaded with them to take the Jews already.

"Why? We agreed that you would keep them for two weeks."

"I refuse to keep them a minute longer. They've been here a week, and already they want to air-condition the place!"

That's who we are. We are what we do. So, you can fully realize the prophet Malachi's mandate for purposeful living in response to God's call. You too can do justice, love mercy, and walk humbly with your God. And, of course, air-condition the place.

You can begin to fulfill these goals. Right now. No waiting required. Because there's no messiah, and you're it.

So, what are you going to do about it?

6

Delayed Gratification

THE OREO COOKIE. That simple, delectable sandwich treat with two chocolate wafers housing that luscious creamy filling. You probably think I'm bringing up this subject because, as a confirmed chocoholic, I need a good excuse to take a break from writing. You're not entirely wrong, but it does seem to me that how you eat an Oreo says a lot about who you are as a person and how you look at the world.

Some people simply pour a large glass of milk and sink their teeth into the whole cookie all at one time. These are the globalists, who believe that the world ought to be united, not divided into separate regions and ideologies. Integrating diverse elements produces a harmony that can have implications for nuclear disarmament, the eradication of poverty, and world peace.

Then, there are the people who take apart the Oreo, who surgically remove the wafer from the filling. These are the nationalists, who see the advantages of one particular approach or another and are intent on celebrating the superiority of one social system over the other. They don't want to mix the elements of the cookie any more than they want their lives sullied by assimilating alternate ways of life into theirs. Can you imagine Judah the Maccabee eating an Oreo whole? No, he would separate out the most desirable parts, keeping each pristine, protecting it from the seductive clutches of majority culture.

Those who want the messiah to come now and who will do

whatever it takes to make it happen would go a step further. Not only would they separate the Oreo—because, after all, who wants to hang around with people and policies that make you miserable—they would eat the filling first! When I asked one of my students why she took the Oreo apart and immediately plunged her whole face into the filling, she looked at me as if I had come from the planet Pluto. "Because it's the best part." Such people eat the best part first and fast, not thinking about the consequences of such rash actions or whether there will be a letdown when all they have left is two average wafers waiting forlornly to be devoured.

THE VALUE OF DELAYED GRATIFICATION

The people who truly inspire me are those who take the exact opposite tack: they eat the filling at the end. They know it's the best part of the whole thing, so, in effect, they are saving the best for last. They see the value of delayed gratification. They are prepared to wait for a higher level of satisfaction than they might have attained had they plunged in at the outset.

That's what the Rabbis of the talmudic age wanted to do about the messiah problem. Messianic fervor was alive and well. Even with the serious threat posed to Judaism by the breakaway messianic movement that would become Christianity, and the tragedies that befell the Jewish people both when the Romans crushed them and destroyed the Temple in 70 C.E. and then when Bar Kokhba's messianic militarism turned into tragic defeat, even so the yearning did not abate. The Rabbis clearly saw a destructive element in the messianic ideal, but they also knew they couldn't curtail the passions of the people by rabbinic fiat. So, brilliantly, they channeled their messianism in a way that didn't dampen the ardor but rather postponed its gratification.

This certainly wasn't the only time the Rabbis took a popular idea that they found to be less than edifying or even threatening to them and to Jewish tradition, and changed the focus. For many centuries,

Jews (and others as well) were extremely superstitious, particularly around important lifecycle, life-changing events. They felt a strong urge to ward off evil spirits threatening their well-being. Women, for example, would often put food under their bed so that the evil spirits would go for these treats and not their vulnerable baby. Some tied a string around their expanded stomach and tied the same string around the grave of a *tzaddik*, a holy man, in the hope that his righteousness would overpower the evil elements lurking about.

Similarly, at a wedding, when men drank a *l'chaim,* they would then throw their glasses against the wall with the hope of scaring off those demonic presences. As you might imagine, this practice did not thrill the Rabbis. They certainly did not want to see sacred practices so suffused with superstition.

These "men of God" couldn't take the "if you can't beat them, join them" approach. Being practical men, however, they took the "if you can't beat them, change them" tack. Break your glass if you must, but understand why you are doing so. We break a glass to remember how shattered we were when the First and Second Temples were destroyed, and we have a responsibility to rebuild the Temple and Judaism through our actions.

SLOWING THE MESSIANIC PACE

That's the Rabbis for you! They didn't throw out the baby with the bath water but found it a new home within a different, sacred, sanctioned context. A key player in channeling messianism was Rabban Gamaliel the Second, who taught in the academy at Yavne. This academy was established after the moderate elements in Israelite leadership brokered a deal with Rome during the crushing war of 66–70. In a daring move, they defied the Zealots who, from within the Temple compound, threatened to destroy any Jew who refused to fight the Romans to the death. These moderates placed the revered Rabbi Johanan ben Zakkai in a coffin and got him past both internal and external checkpoints to negotiate a deal with Rome: we will defy our own radicals and lay down arms in exchange for the right to survive and teach Torah to the next generation. So, a citadel of Jewish learning was established at Yavne to provide stability and continuity to a people who too often craved messianic immediacy.

Some years later at Yavne, Gamaliel continued the process of centralizing and structuring prayer liturgy, which had begun at least a generation earlier. If the Temple was no longer to be the place and means of worshipping God, another way of communicating with the Holy One had to be established. In the decades following the destruction, Rabbis had helped the people create a prayer experience with two crucial components. First, the central profession of faith, the *Sh'ma,* found in the Book of Deuteronomy, was flanked by blessings acknowledging God's central role in creation, revelation of Torah, and redemption of our people from slavery. Second, the more personal entreaties called the *Amidah* (the standing prayer) were blessings of praise and thanksgiving but also of petition to God. As you can imagine, these were more freewheeling, subject to personal needs and communal custom. Gamaliel saw the importance of providing order to these blessings within Jewish prayer so that communities could be more united in their approach to God and Jewish tradition. So, at Yavne, he arranged these blessings into the *Sh'moneh Esreh,* an ordered eighteen-blessing prayer unit (for a more comprehensive understanding of the blessings in the *Amidah,* see *My People's Prayer Book: The Amidah* edited by Dr. Lawrence A. Hoffman and published by Jewish Lights).

The themes of the intermediary blessings of the *Amidah,* those which are petitionary to God rather than praising of God, are extremely interesting to look at. They are, in order:

4. Wisdom

5. Repentance

6. Forgiveness

7. Deliverance

8. Healing

9. Agricultural abundance

10. The ingathering of the exiles

11. Justice

12. The punishment of heretics

13. Reward of the righteous

14. Rebuilding of Jerusalem

15. Restoration of David to the messianic throne

16. Appreciation to God for hearing and heeding prayer

The list immediately prompts questions: Why were these particular themes chosen? What is the connection between the blessings? Is there a progression here that gets us to a particular emotion or resolve? Given the fact that the *Amidah* prayer rubrics are more personal than those in the *Sh'ma,* there still seems to be a greater emphasis on communal needs than on personal needs. To put it another way, our prayer experience take us from the more private to the more public. The *Amidah* seems to be teaching that the acquisition of wisdom will lead to repentance, from which will emerge forgiveness. Forgiveness on a grand scale, in turn, can lead to a redemption or deliverance from patterned ways, and a genuine healing can take place from which rewards like an abundance of food can become manifest.

THE AMIDAH AS MESSIANIC CHECKLIST

It seems quite possible, then, that in the order of these blessings, Gamaliel was trying to accomplish an important purpose. The goal of these petitionary entreaties seems to be the ingathering of the exiles, the restoration of true justice, proper reward and punishment for actions, the rebuilding of Jerusalem and the Temple, and, finally, the installing of the rightful descendant of King David to the messianic throne.

So, the *Amidah* appears to be no mere spiritual document, no quiet opportunity for a people to interact with their God. The *Amidah* is first and foremost a political manifesto, urging personal responsibility upon the worshiper that will lead to a communal, redemptive cleansing, preparing us for the coming of the messiah.

Missing here is any sense of the painful instability the prophets warned would precede the messianic era. No call to militancy is found in these blessings. Rather, an alternative means of achieving the same ends is presented. Gamaliel seems to argue that taking up arms to hasten the coming of the messiah is not only foolhardy; it will have tragic implications. Look at the defeats we suffered at the hands of Rome. Yes, there is much we can do to prepare the ground; perhaps what we do is vital precondition. But, ultimately, God will bring the messiah at a time and circumstance of divine, not human, choosing.

My brilliant teacher of liturgy, Dr. Lawrence A. Hoffman, professor at Hebrew Union College–Jewish Institute of Religion, using the groundbreaking work of his teacher, Professor Leon Liebriech, believes that Gamaliel had something else in mind besides preaching that redemption will come through spiritual rather than military means. Gamaliel here has produced a type of messianic checklist for all aspirants to the throne. You say you are the messiah and that I should drop everything and follow you in a faithful quest? Well, has repentance in fact happened? Has there been a collective healing, which has produced agricultural prosperity? This surely would provide a more objective way to judge would-be messiahs.

CHANNELED MESSIANISM

Gamaliel produces a channeled messianism in this prayer rubric. No, you should not quash your dreams for the messianic era, but you do have some means beyond visceral passion for judging between a true and a false messiah. If a candidate can't produce some results, he should desist from messianic pretensions before he causes harm and drains the lifeblood of hope from our people (*The Amidah*, pp. 17–36).

In counseling delayed gratification here, Gamaliel is teaching something quite profound. You don't have to sit back and wait passively for the messiah to come. Nor do you have to rush impulsively into military battle. You can do the quiet work of acquiring wisdom, doing *teshuvah*, forgiving others, helping collective healing one *mitzvah* at a time. Not only will you be doing messianic work, but you will be filling your life with purpose in achieving a righteousness and *mentschlichtkeit*, acting with true kindness and caring, for which you were created in the first place.

The notion of the messianic checklist reminds me of a young woman I'll call Sharon, who came to my study to ask an important, and, for her, painful question: "Why are there no great Jewish guys out there?" She proceeded to regale me with her efforts to find a suitable boyfriend: singles events, Internet dating services, synagogues, fix-ups. She told me of some of her disastrous first dates. "You know the dating organization 'It's Just Lunch'? My blind dates have been so horrendous I won't waste a whole lunch on these guys. In fact, if we meet for coffee, I insist that it is iced.

"So, in despair, I made a little checklist of what I am looking for. Believe me, it's not about getting a three-car garage and a guy with a six-pack stomach. Do you want to hear the list?"

Before I could answer, she continued,

"Well, Rabbi, here it is."

How many times does he say "I" in the first five minutes?

Does he ask any questions about me?

Does he discuss his family or is he a lone ranger?

Is he comfortable being a Jew?

Has he grown up yet?

Is he a *mentsch*?

When I protested that what draws people together is not getting enough checks but the less exacting search for a personal chemistry, she put up her hand. "I know, Rabbi, but I do this more for me than for him. When I was in high school and college and even beyond, I slept with so many guys I barely knew. I didn't have sex with them because I particularly liked them, but because I didn't value myself enough. In my mind I wasn't worthy of love, so I freely lent out my body. Who would want me for any other reason? But I was so unhappy."

I saw her several times over the next year. On the next visit she told me she had done some things to address her problem. "I began to work out, see a therapist, and—you won't believe this, Rabbi—I went to a great Torah study for singles." She seemed more relaxed, more in charge.

Next time I saw her, she was all smiles. "I met someone, Rabbi. It's early, and I'm not sure where it is going, but he's really special."

"Did he get enough check marks?" I couldn't resist asking the question.

"Funny thing about that! After I met with you, Rabbi, I continued to use that checklist. But I applied it to myself. It helped me become the kind of person I could respect and hopefully that someone would love."

YOUR MESSIANIC POTENTIAL

Often it's nice to resist the temptation to rush headlong to fulfill your ambitions. Slowing down, you can assess the wisdom of the goal and figure out your role in creating that particular miracle. That's the wisdom in the rabbinic teaching that if someone comes to tell you that the messiah is coming while you are planting a tree, you should finish planting the tree and then go to greet the messiah. So my advice here is this: Slow down. Take a deep breath. Appreciate life and appreciate what you can do with your wondrous potential.

In his book *When All You Ever Wanted Isn't Enough*, Rabbi Harold Kushner tells the story of a rabbi who once asked a prominent member of his congregation,

"Whenever I see you, you're always in a hurry. Tell me, where are you running all the time?"

The man answered, "I'm running after success, I'm running after fulfillment, I'm running after the reward for all my hard work."

The rabbi responded, "That's a good answer if you assume that all those blessings are somewhere ahead of you, trying to elude you and if you run fast enough, you may catch up with them. But isn't it possible that those blessings are behind you, that they are looking for you, and the more you run, the harder you make it for them to find you?"

Isn't it possible indeed that God has all sorts of wonderful presents for us—good food and beautiful sunsets and flowers budding in the spring and leaves turning in the fall and quiet moments of sharing—but we in our pursuit of happiness are so constantly on the go that He can't find us at home to deliver them? (*When All You've Ever Wanted Isn't Enough,* p. 146).

SUFFERING IS A GREAT TEACHER

Sometimes the greatest teacher of wisdom is serious illness, even death. In these life-changing events, we are forced to slow down, climb off the ladder, abandon our checklist of pulsating productivity, and consider what really matters. Rabbi Harold Schulweis, whom I introduced earlier in this book, discusses what he learned while lying in a hospital bed after a coronary:

> In time, the patient will learn not to be driven by omnivorous conceits or wild discontents. He will learn this of himself; no one else will teach him to learn to live with a proportionate ambition. But his danger lies in invalidating life by acting the invalid. He must not "play possum," pretend not to be alive in order to gain immortality. Life must be lived with passion, *b'chol l'vovocha u'v-chol nafshecha, u'vchol m'odecha,* with all your heart and with all your soul and with all your might. Otherwise existence is at best a quantitative prolongation.
>
> When the debris and the clutter of the armored self clear away you may begin your rediscovery. Old-new questions reappear. What and who and when is most important in your life? These questions call for self-revelation and for confessional. This moment, this hour, this day is most important. Do you know whether you will have another like this one? Do not neglect the present tense. And this one sitting beside your bed. Will there be another like this one? No book held in my hand but this human hand held in mine makes me strong, helps me struggle against submission.
>
> We need not wait for a calamitous event to open our eyes to this hour and to those who are about us. Recovery is a return. Go home to your families and love them. Go home to your houses and with your Sabbath lights and wine and white challah make peace. Go home to your families and bind the

injured relations. Cast aside invective and sharpness of tongue and irony and sarcasm and judgment and blame. Go home to your family and learn to listen and enjoy and share legend and story and laugh together, sing together and study together and come to shul together. And go home to your friends. Do not let small things, jealousies, demeaning envies destroy the health in your life (*Moment,* November 1981, p. 46).

The messiah doesn't have to come for you to acquire the perspective to live the way you have always wanted to live. Thank God, in fact, that the messiah doesn't come so quickly, so you can have something to work for, so you can set messianic goals of making your life and someone else's better than it has been before.

In the slow, steady, spectacular growth that can accompany wisdom, you can pray the blessings of the *Amidah* and see how much you still have to do and how much you can contribute to the fruition of these hopes, which will lead to a better world. Probably no one person will ever burst on the world scene who can achieve the goals set forth in these messianic blessings. But that is precisely the point. It is not for someone else to do the work. It is for you, me, and everyone else, because there is no messiah and you're it.

ONE OF YOU IS THE MESSIAH

The story is told about a monastery that had fallen upon hard times. Only five monks lived there, and all were over seventy years of age. In the deep woods surrounding the monastery was a little hut, which a rabbi from a nearby town occasionally used for a retreat. Through years of prayer and contemplation, the old monks had become a bit psychic, so they could always sense when the rabbi was there.

"The rabbi is in the woods, the rabbi is in the woods," they whispered to one another.

As he agonized over the imminent death of his order, it occurred to the abbot to visit the rabbi to see whether he could offer any advice to save the monastery.

"Is there anything you can tell me?"

"No, I am sorry," the rabbi responded. "I have no advice to give. The only thing I can tell you is that one of you is the messiah."

When the abbot returned to the monastery, his fellow monks gathered around. "Well, what did the rabbi say?"

"He couldn't help. We just wept together and read Torah. The only thing he could say, just as I was leaving, was that one of us was the messiah. I don't know what that means."

In the months that followed, the monks pondered his words. One of us is the messiah. Could he have meant one of us in the monastery? If so, which one? The abbot? He has been our teacher for more than a generation. Brother Thomas? For sure he is a holy man. Brother Eldred? He gets crotchety at times. But come to think of it, even though he is a thorn in people's sides, he's virtually always right. Surely not Brother Phillip. He is passive, a real nobody. But then, he has a gift for somehow always being there when you need him. Of course the rabbi didn't mean me. He couldn't possibly have meant me. I'm just an ordinary person. Yet, supposing he did? Suppose I am the messiah? Oh God, not me. I couldn't be it, could I?

As they contemplated the matter the old monks began to treat one another with extraordinary respect on the off chance that one of them might, in fact, be the messiah. It so happened that people from the town still visited the monastery from time to time because of its beautiful location. People began to sense a real change of mood there. The aura of extraordinary solicitude that the five monks extended to one another began to be felt by the visitors as well.

In time, more people began to come to picnic, pray, and play. Even some young men came and talked with the old monks. In fact, some of them even asked to join the monastery. Within a few years, the monastery had once again become a thriving order, a center of light and spirituality, thanks to the rabbi's gift.

The messiah is one of you. So you can stop running to find out what you already have. Stop looking for instant gratification, for you possess the longer-term potential for true satisfaction within. Stop manufacturing fleeting, shortsighted goals, for the best goal of all already comes with your title.

You are the messiah. And there is really a lot you can do about that.

7

What Should the Messiah Look Like?

THE RABBIS WHO were responsible for the Talmud compiled in both Jerusalem and Babylonia had the opportunity not only to raise the bar on messianic candidates, expecting them to produce the results of a saved world before assuming the messianic mantle, but to practically eliminate such speculation altogether. After all, those descendants of the pharisaic tradition had won the battle to establish their authority in the Jewish community, thus marginalizing all societal forces who insisted on being strict constitutionalists, recognizing only the written Torah as authoritative.

These Pharisees were able to help adapt Judaism's message and to syncretize our tradition with the best of Greco-Roman and Persian cultures. More to the point, they were in a position to champion God's dominion for people who had reason to skeptically struggle with their own theodicy, their own understanding of why evil exists in the world. To this end, they refocused the ever-changing myth that is Judaism, retelling our story to place emphasis where they felt it belonged.

THE POWER OF A CHANGING MESSIANISM

In a most famous example, it was the Rabbis in Tractate Shabbat, of all places, who asked *"mai Chanukah?"* (What is Chanukah all about?) and proceeded to tell the spellbinding tale of the tiny flask of oil that burned for eight days. God was the author and progenitor of the miracle, they asserted, not Judah the Maccabee or any other human being. Trust in God; anyone else will lead you astray—perhaps tragically so.

If they were successful in recasting one of the great stories of Jewish lore and stripping even Judah the Maccabee of some heroic luster, could they not have debunked the messianic pursuit as an idle, even destructive fantasy? With the Bar Kokhba disaster fresh in mind, and their efforts to cool the ardor for immediate messianic results already bearing fruit, they most probably could have gone all the way and reasserted the sole authority of God to bring forth salvation with no need of any human help. If they didn't want to take this ultimate step, they could have acted as decisively as they did with Chanukah to create a messianic person far less militant and more God-fearing than Bar Kokhba had been.

A NEW FACE FOR THE MESSIAH

In fact, they did neither. This seems to testify to the enduring power of the messianic idea to survive the counterfeits who have surfaced throughout history, as well as the ongoing difficulty our tradition confronted to paint an authoritative picture of the authentic messianic personality.

In fact, it is true that while some Christians often have a predetermined sense of what the messiah did and will look like, Jews consistently have had a difficult time conjuring up a true image of the messiah. As famed scholar Gershom Scholem puts it, "Unlike Christian or Shiite messianism, no memories of a real person are at work here. . .Jesus or the Hidden Imam, who once existed as persons, possess the unmistakable and unforgettable qualities of a person. This is just what the Jewish image of the messiah, by its nature, cannot have, since it can picture everything personal only in completely abstract fashion, having as yet no living experience on which to base it" (Scholem, *Messianic Ideas in Judaism*, pp. 17–18).

TRADITIONAL PICTURES OF THE MESSIAH IN JUDAISM

You might expect a Jewish messianic portrait to be based on the mighty King David. This charismatic ruler so captured the imagination of present and future generations that whoever the messiah will be and whenever he will come, one non-negotiable criterion is that he will be—or at least claim to be—descended from the household of David.

But even there, competing views have intruded. Jewish tradition knows of a Messiah ben Yoseph: "Messiah son of Joseph." According to some texts, this is the messiah who preceded Messiah ben David, and one who suffered defeat in apocalyptic battles that did not lead to redemption. Messiah ben Yosef is presented cryptically in the Talmud: "Our Rabbis taught, the Holy One, blessed be He, will say to the Messiah son of David, 'Ask of me anything and I will give it to thee. . . .' But when this messiah sees that the Messiah son of Joseph was slain, he will say only, 'Lord of the universe, I ask of thee only the gift of life'" (Talmud, *Sukkah* 52a).

The appearance of consecutive messiahs seems to address the question of how such a figure could be present on the world stage without redemption taking place. One messiah's defeat gave birth to the next one, who ultimately could defeat the forces of evil and help redeem humanity. The talmudic text gives further vent to the Rabbis' discomfort with Apocalypse as the necessary precondition to the messiah. Not only are ultimate battles between the forces of good and evil not required for the coming of the messiah, they can even set back the whole enterprise.

It is interesting to note that the concept of Messiah son of

Joseph did not perish in apocalyptic flames. He was reborn in later kabbalistic tradition when Isaac Luria (1534–1572) was identified by the nineteenth-century kabbalist Hayim Vital as Messiah son of Joseph. One of Vital's last disciples, Hayyim ha-Kohen of Aleppo, wrote, "The redeemer of Israel will be marked by two signs: He will be a man of pain and also that he will always and permanently suffer and be acquainted with disease. The meaning of 'man of pain' is that he will always be suffering from a specific disease, which was the case with his (Vital's) master Isaac Luria of blessed memory" (Hayyim ha-Kohen, *Torat Hakham*, fol. 17d). Luria, in fact, died at the age of thirty-eight, victim of an epidemic. The disciples of Luria also kept alive the flickering tradition that the Messiah of the House of Joseph is reborn in every generation. They believed that if there are a sufficient number of righteous men in his generation, then he will be saved from death by their merit, but if no one possesses such merit, then he must die. By the repeated death he suffers in every generation, he atones for himself so that he may die every time by a divine kiss (Nathan Shapira as quoted in Scholem's *Sabbatai Sevi*, pp. 54–55).

SWASHBUCKLING MESSIAH

The image of the defeated, dying man of pain and disease did not prevail in Jewish messianic thinking. The Talmud's more popular image of a powerful, swashbuckling military leader, interestingly enough, is personified less by King David than by King Hezekiah. Hezekiah was a charismatic young king in the eighth century B.C.E., who was twenty-five years old when he began to reign in the southern kingdom of Judah and who kept his throne for twenty-nine years. Among his first royal acts was to destroy the shrines built by his own people to commit idolatry. Next, he commanded the forces who defeated the Philistines and battled the scourge of the north, Assyria, which had set designs on Jerusalem. The Hebrew Bible heaps high praise on the young ruler: "He trusted in the Lord, God of Israel, so before and after his throne, there were no kings of Judah like him. For he cleaved to the Lord and departed not from following Him, but kept his commandments which the Lord had commanded Moses. And God was with him, and he prospered in every endeavor he undertook" (I Kings, Chapter 18).

Once having established that Hezekiah had the proper bloodlines for messianic work, that he was descended from the House of David, the Rabbis dutifully embraced him as a messianic candidate. He had it all: true righteousness, faith in God, military acumen, and both the passion to fight idolatry and the means to do something about it. Moreover, he lacked the moral shortcomings that had cost David the right to build the Temple in Jerusalem in the first place.

So attractive a messianic possibility was Hezekiah that the first-century rabbinic luminary Rabbi Johanan ben Zakkai at the point of death saw a vision of Hezekiah coming to greet him and urged his people to prepare a throne for the messianic king, as it is written, "Clear the house of defilement and set a throne for Hezekiah, King of Judah" (Palestinian Talmud, *Sotah* 9:17).

MESSIAH IS IN EVERY GENERATION

The Talmud's intrigue with Hezekiah as messiah sparked the imagination of latter kabbalists, who believed that in fact God sends a spark of the messiah-soul into the world in every generation. Its function is to redeem Israel if we are worthy—or at least to preserve the world in evil times. A popular book of the late sixteenth century *Tuv ha-Aretz,* by Nathan Shpira of Jerusalem, posits that "in every generation God creates a perfectly righteous man worthy—like Moses—on whom the *Shekhinah* rests, provided that also his generation merits it" (fol. 38a). Though a spark exists in every generation, the highest part of the soul comes to the anointed one only after the world has experienced its ultimate readiness for the restorative process, called *tikkun*. Only the actual messiah, chosen by God, receives this crucial piece of soulfulness.

As compelling as these images are, no single one so captures the popular or rabbinic imagination as to constitute a set view of what the messiah ultimately will look like. The field remained wide open to learned speculation. For example, the prophet Zechariah understood that a king would arrive to lift the people out of despair. "Behold thy king comes unto thee, he is just, embodying salvation, yet so lowly that he arrives upon an ass" (Zechariah 9:9). On the basis of this text, Rav Joseph could exclaim with unbridled enthusiasm, "Let the messiah come, and may I be privileged to sit in the shadow of the dung of his ass" (*Sanhedrin* 98b).

The famed medieval scholar Maimonides wanted both to sever the connection between the messiah and any apocalyptic precedents and to debunk the notion that the messiah would have a particular appearance. Neither the dashing man about town nor the lowly figure riding on an ass captured his imagination. He was much more interested in what the messiah would do than in what he would look like. Maimonides' views will be examined at length in the next chapter.

DYSFUNCTIONAL MESSIAH

Jewish history has proved that if the circumstances are right, people will even embrace a messiah who appears totally delusional, manifesting behavior that is shocking to behold. Sabbatai Tzvi, who has been called a manic-depressive psychotic, nonetheless galvanized most of the Jewish world, leaders of society and the population at large, in both East and West. Extremely charismatic, Sabbatai could comport himself with quiet dignity, assuming the pose of nobility.

Yet, his public outbursts, which included blasphemies, and his open flaunting of Torah law fit the profile of someone we would commit to a long-term treatment program, not someone we would embrace as the anointed one of God.

One incident, briefly told, will suffice to illustrate this point. On the Shabbat of December 12, 1665, Sabbatai, upset that an "infidel," or Temple leader who had criticized him, was not ejected from the synagogue, marched to the synagogue with five hundred followers. Finding the doors closed, he took an ax and smashed the gates.

After reading from the Torah, Sabbatai cupped his hands to his mouth and trumpeted in the direction of the four winds. Then he expanded upon the kabbalistic reason for his desecration of the Sabbath, saying, "It is time to work for the Lord, (therefore) the law may be transgressed." He reviled and insulted the Rabbis. Then, after his sermon, Sabbatai went up to the ark and, with the Torah scroll in his arms, sang his favorite song— an ancient Castilian love ballad, "Meliseldi," the story of the lover who lay with the emperor's daughter. This was, for Sabbatai, a mystical allegory in which he was like a bridegroom, husband of the beloved Torah, who was no other than the divine *Shekhinah* herself (*Sabbatai Sevi*, pp. 400–401).

Another, much more "normal" and compelling image of the messiah, is found in the Talmud. Its power is self-evident. Rabbi Joshua ben Levi met Elijah the prophet at the entrance of Rabbi Simeon bar Yohai's burial cave and asked him a crucial question:

"When will the messiah come?"

"Go and ask him yourself," Elijah responded.

"Ask him myself? Where does he live?"

"At the entrance to Rome, in front of the gate."

"How will I recognize him?"

"He sits among the lepers. They tie and untie the bandages all at once. He unties and reties them one at a time."

So, Joshua ben Levi went to the gate and located him.

"Peace be upon you, O son of Levi! When will the master come?"

"Today!"

Incredulous, Joshua ben Levi ran back to Elijah to tell him the tale. Said Elijah to him, "He just assured you and your father a place in the world to come." "Then he lied to me," contested Joshua, "for he told me the messiah would come today, yet he did not come."

Said Elijah to him, "This is what he meant. He will come today if you hearken to His voice" (*Sanhedrin* 98a).

THE MESSIAH IS AMONG US

This talmudic tale speaks powerfully to us, for it places the messiah where we would like him to be—here, in our world, rolling up his sleeves and plunging into the world of human pain and suffering. The messiah is already among us, doing good works, contends this text. Yet, he must still be activated by us. If we respond to this compelling voice and do God's will, do what we are capable of, be all we were created to be, the messiah will come—even today.

This story clearly reinforces the message of this book. There's no need to yearn for some transcendent figure who will do for us only what we can do for ourselves. Moreover, it is much too seductive to look for some suave, macho figure who will rescue us from ourselves and who, in one sweep of the cape, can replace reality with fantasy. The bravado of such figures and their bad-boy image often camouflages the fact that they themselves are in need of rescue. Though this can be attractive to people with nurturing instincts, such a scenario, while it may lead to momentary exhilaration and passion, will more than likely end in long-term disappointment and despair.

Rescuing someone by attempting to recreate that person in our image is daunting work. Searching for such people leads us astray. We have to do the work of self-improvement and restoration ourselves. No redeemer can do that for us. And for the community as a whole, judging a redeemer not by initial appearance but by results achieved over the long haul seems to be wise counsel for every situation.

KEEPING THE MESSIANIC QUEST ALIVE

The Rabbis of the Talmud, who, more than any other force, shifted Judaism's paradigm from a strong, centralized priestly authority to a more diffuse, democratic one in which they could empower the people to develop their own relationship with God, had a good reason not to destroy the messianic quest. But now, each of us has to become God's covenantal partner. In helping bring on the messiah, each of us can help God as well. All of us potentially should be soldiers fighting against both human evil and false messiahs. If they didn't yet know what the messiah would look like, the Rabbis knew what they didn't want the messiah to act like. They made sure that their people and their descendants would know it too.

8

You'll Know Him after You See Him: Maimonides' Messiah

J EWS HAVE OFTEN SOUGHT to reconcile the seemingly irreconcilable. They have searched for answers to life's most profound questions: If God is good, why is there evil? If God is all-powerful, why were the "chosen people" seemingly so powerless? In their desperate search for answers, for Truth in a world where they have all too often fallen victim to dangerously false doctrines, they have clung to the lessons learned from Scripture through ongoing immersion in the text. So, the Torah teaches that the God of Israel, who redeemed our people from Egypt in a mighty battle between the forces of good and evil, is active in human history and will continue to save us.

Jews have always understood that the battle waged against evil is not an easy one. God seemingly could not accomplish salvation from Egyptian oppression without the intercession of Moses. Help, then, may have to come from a similar source today. So, while they were buffeted by external enemies and sometimes led astray by their own leaders, who often did not deliver what they promised, they clung to any embodiment, any slightly creditable reenactment of God's providence in history. Even a new round of messiahs could take the people on flights of fancy, because whimsical journeys seemed to offer more promise than the numbing, pain-seared present.

Those who wanted to keep their feet on the ground, however, and who wanted to fix their gaze not on some distant horizon of wholly transformed reality but squarely on this world, in the hope of surviving and even improving on their lot, could find support from Judaism's greatest philosopher. He revolutionized how a Jew could read the Bible, and then he single-handedly made it possible to shift the focus from an other-worldly orientation to a reality-based concentration on the here and now.

Moses Maimonides, known as Rambam for the acronym Rabbi Moses Ben Maimon (1135–1204), was born in Spain, ended his life in Israel and Egypt, and lived among the competing and intersecting ideas of Judaism, Islam, and Christianity. He was an Aristotelian and thus felt compelled to navigate the relationship between faith and reason. He was no apologist for Judaism, but he was ever conscious not only of competing philosophical systems but of very real pressures on Jews to convert to Islam or Christianity. Much of his philosophical work was elitist and was therefore designed to keep our own intellects in the Jewish fold and to fend off those who regarded Judaism as overly reliant on truths the mind could not rationally or scientifically discern.

MAIMONIDES' RATIONAL, NON-INTERCESSIONARY GOD

Scriptural accounts of God's involvement in creation and revelation, therefore, could never contradict reason. Whereas the Torah assumes divine existence, introducing God as creator of the world without a philosophical proof text, Maimonides in his major philosophical work, *The Guide to the Perplexed*, launched into "scientific" proofs of God's existence. For example, everything in the world moves and changes; these moves are caused by another force-producing motion. But there is a logical end to that chain. There is a sphere that produces motion in others but is not moved by another mover. This prime mover Maimonides calls God. Consistent with reason, Maimonides' God parts company with the biblical portrait of a God who speaks, gets angry, and interferes mightily in the affairs of humankind. This is made clear in Maimonides' interpretation of God's self-description to Moses as *Ehyeh Asher Ehyeh* (Exodus 3:14). When Moses asserts the need to have some way to introduce God to his own people back in Egypt, this is the answer ascribed to God. The translations *I will be who I will be* or *I am that I am* generally are taken to mean that God will be responsive to the suffering of the Jewish people and thus will be either ever-present or present as needed.

Maimonides has a different, decidedly more rational take. God here is not a "personal" presence but is a necessary existent:

> For at that time only a righteous few were aware of the existence of the deity, and to the extent they could appertain God, they still could not separate themselves from things perceived by the senses and thus had not obtained intellectual perfection. Accordingly, God made known [to Moses] the knowledge that he was to convey to them and through which they would acquire a true notion of the existence of God, this knowledge being: *I am that I am.* This is a name deriving from the verb to be, *hayah,* which signifies existence.
>
> Scripture makes, as it were, a clear statement that He is existent not through existence. Rather, there is a necessarily existent power, that has never been, or ever will be, non-existent (*The Guide to the Perplexed* 1:63).

God as necessary existent for anything else to exist is a basic philosophical principle for Rambam. This interpretation establishes divine perfection and self-sufficiency but does not paint a picture of a personal deity active in the affairs and redemption of humankind. People can't know that much about God.

Statements describing God's mercy or compassion are human projections about God, not actual divine attributes. Here Maimonides adapts a "negative" theology. All we can know, for instance, is not that God exists but that God is not nonexistent.

The coming of the messiah is clearly a central belief for Maimonides. In fact, this is the twelfth of his "Thirteen Principles" in his commentary on the Mishnah to help rank-and-file Jews determine the core truths of their faith. This concept appeared in an expanded creedal form, probably first in the *Venice Haggadah* in 1566, as "I believe with perfect faith in the coming of the messiah. Even though he may tarry, still I do believe." These words, later put to music, resonated deeply in the souls of many Jews and were on the lips of some believers as they went to their deaths during the Holocaust.

Yet, it still should come as no surprise to learn that Maimonides' messiah was not "heaven sent." His is not a God who would send an only son to earth or, for that matter, any other redeemer in the divine name to rescue humanity from itself.

NORMALCY IN THE MESSIANIC IDEA

The messiah, in Rambam's world, is decidedly human, with a very this-worldly mission. Transcending our world as we know it is not the goal. We are not to be airlifted to another place or time. Rather, transformation of the world will take place in this way:

> Do not suppose that King Messiah will have to perform signs and wonders, create new things in the world, revive the dead or similar acts. It is not so. If a king will arrive from the house of David, a student of Torah, performing good deeds like his ancestor David. . .and prevail upon all Israel to reinstate the Torah and to follow its direction, and will fight the battle of the Lord, he will presumably be the messiah. If he has done these

things and succeeded, having overcome the surrounding enemy nations and rebuilt the sanctuary on its site and gathered the dispersed of Israel, he will already be the messiah. If he has not succeeded to such an extent, or has been slain, it is certain that he is not the one concerning whom the Torah has assured us (*Mishneh Torah,* Kings, Chapter 11).

This is a remarkable text in several respects. Notice that no apocalyptic event needs to happen before the messiah appears. Such dramatic and unsettling messianic explosions give way to a calmer, more evolutionary process in Rambam's work. Nothing spectacular or extraordinary needs to take place. The world does not have to shake. All people can be the messiah if they truly wish. Every virtuous king of Israel, in fact, should have messianic goals on his agenda. No preordaining or foretelling of arrival needs to occur.

THE MESSIAH IS JUDGED BY RESULTS

What distinguishes the messiah from others, in Maimonides' view, is results. In other words, we will know of the coming of the messiah not because of painful apocalyptic events that shake the world to the core. On the contrary, we will find the messiah when all the teachings laid out in the Hebrew Bible are followed and we are back on our Land, having rebuilt the Temple and gathered in the exiles, and are living a life of Torah.

The effects of the messiah's coming are more political than personal. The resulting restoration of a people to its home and traditional ways will engender a greater sense of security, enabling them to fulfill their spiritual potential. But no brave new world is contemplated. Torah remains the constitution, the guide, the quest. But human beings still are left with the greatest gift bestowed upon us at the moment of creation: personal choice. Maimonides fought against any suggestion that history is determined by a fixed, divine blueprint. Moral struggle is a human imperative preordained by God. Nor does the coming of the messiah take that privilege, that burden from us. As professor Gershom Scholem contended, "Maimonides nowhere recognizes a causal relationship between the coming of the messiah and human conduct. It is not Israel's repentance which brings about redemption. . ." (*Messianic Idea*, pp. 30–31).

I am not at all sure that Maimonides would fully agree with Scholem. For if God is found in the ideal of perfection for our world, laid out at the time of revelation, it is our task to respond to that ideal and thus overcome the temptation to immorality. So, in this sense, there does seem to be a very real causal relationship between human action and the coming of the messiah. Results are the determining factor of success, and no "messianic" leaders are going to succeed unilaterally. They can lay out the vision and set the standard, but if the people don't respond, change their ways, and rise to their fullest potential, no leader of Israel ever can achieve messianic results.

So, for Maimonides no supernatural figure will suddenly appear to change the world as we know it. The world will have the same physical contours it has always had. People will have the same physical properties and moral challenges as before. No moral transplant, no new human nature will be grafted onto us. Messianism doesn't do that for us, in Maimonides' view of the cosmos. As modern Orthodox theologian Dr. David Hartman puts it: "Messianism is not a final resolution to the struggle of human history; it is a realistically possible state of affairs which provides for the unleashing of human spiritual capacities and the baring of new and undreamed of personal aspirations" (*Joy and Responsibility*, p. 249).

WE WILL BRING ON THE MESSIAH

Leaders may inspire, but in the end we must follow. You and I will struggle with the very real temptation to be less than we can be, to lower our sights to popular norms. But, as I will suggest in subsequent chapters, the Jewish people have survived all attempts to destroy not only their bodies but their souls as well, to lay waste their dreams, to mock their ideals for a more just and fair world. We have not been made footnotes to history, despite the best efforts of our many foes. We have remained players, actors on the world stage, partners in the quest for human redemption. We can teach the world how to hold onto light in the face of darkness, breed hope in the face of despair. We can make the messianic happen.

In fact, it cannot happen without us. In Dr. David Hartman's words: "If Maimonides is right, then the comfort provided by religious hope need not be based on discontinuous ruptures in history. Man bears witness to God's presence in history by persevering in the struggle for justice" (Ibid, p.256).

It's a messianic struggle for justice.

Ours.

9

Kabbalah's Call: We Are the Messiah

M AIMONIDES' MESSIAH does not anticipate apocalyptic upheaval in the world preceding his arrival. What a relief for
Jews who wanted a redeemed world but didn't want it or themselves destroyed along the way. Maimonides thus calms the messianic waters by "normalizing" and even politicizing the process.
No predestination is required of the candidate. God does not
invest supernatural qualities in a person, then send that person
down to accomplish divinely ordained actions. The messiah, to
Rambam, is a human being who possesses superb leadership abilities to accomplish the goals the Jewish people yearn for, which
they have inherited from their textual tradition and historic con-
sciousness.

This messiah appears to a normal world in a most ordinary
way. You don't even know a messiah when you see one. You know
the messiah only after the fact. Someone is a true messiah only
if that individual accomplishes messianic results. As we have
seen, this concept is most attractive to those who yearn for a better world but who fear the shaking of the earth to its core in the
ultimate battle between the forces of good and evil that presage
the coming of the messiah in much of Jewish tradition.

But, what do you do if your world already has been shaken to
the core? What if you don't have to imagine tumult, desolation,

and dislocation because they are all around you? If you possess a searing faith in God and spend your waking hours contemplating ways to bridge the distance between the divine and human realms in the hope of getting even a bit closer to God's essence, but then you are uprooted from your home and exiled from your land, you need to find a new explanation for your spectacularly changed circumstances.

LURIANIC KABBALISTS SEEK REASONS FOR SUFFERING

This was the situation for a small group of kabbalists who banded together in the mid-sixteenth century in the northern Galilee town of Safed to assess where they had been, what had happened to them, and how to pick up the pieces of their shattered lives and their shattered world.

Their mystical speculations constituted a dramatic change in focus for kabbalah. From its heyday in the twelfth century until the expulsion from Spain in 1492, kabbalah was centered more on the individual than on the community, more on matters of personal redemption and uplift than on cosmic chaos. Kabbalists had plunged deeply into the mystery of creation, not just to seek answers to great questions inherent in the universe but, more importantly, to ascend the ladder of spiritual rungs that links the two worlds, so that they could escape the imperfections of the world as they knew them and climb up into the bliss of the divine presence.

The centerpiece of Spanish kabbalah, the *Zohar*, composed in the last quarter of the thirteenth century in Castile, Spain, postulates that God makes this ascent possible through the gift of divine light gradually illuminating the world. This light brought by the messiah slowly lifts the righteous Israelites out of *galut*, or exile, and brings them to a state of redemption. This sunny, optimistic view of what each of us can hope to expect, and the collective redemption possible as a result, later seemed hope-lessly naïve to the mystics, who had to be still reeling from the catastrophe of 1492.

At first, kabbalists had a ready explanation for these shatter-ing events, one that generated a great deal of excitement through-out the Jewish world: the Apocalypse—the necessary pre-condition for the coming of the messiah—had arrived. Suffering was clearly at hand, but wasn't that what the prophets had predicted? They were experiencing the birth pangs of the messiah and thus should exult in the glories of the anticipated, splendid new age.

But redemption did not come, only dislocation and disillu-sionment. The promise of a new age gave way to the promise of an uncertain future. What had happened? Who was to blame? What could they do now?

Many were the explanations formulated by this group of mystics in sixteenth-century Safed. One system of thought cap-tured their imagination more than any other and ultimately came to hold sway with the Jewish people as a whole. It was for-mulated by the intense and introverted Rabbi Isaac Luria (1534–1572), later called *Ha-Ari* (the Lion), and came to be known as Lurianic kabbalah. Luria's radical visions and beliefs were never published but were conveyed orally to his disciples, prin-cipally Hayim Vital and Joseph ibn T'bul, who jealously guarded their notes and did not permit them to see the light of day. Only at the end of Vital's life was a manuscript published in Europe, much against Vital's wishes. We will never know how much of Luria's system underwent emendation by his zealous students (*Sabbatai Sevi*, p. 24).

Luria's teachings sought to explain not only their current existential situation but, more globally, to understand the state of being of the entire world. These were drastic times, calling for drastic explanations. Luria certainly provided one. To do so, Luria had to go back to prehistoric time, to the beginning of all creation.

The world, in Luria's view, began with a stunning divine concession. God was everything and everywhere, filling all primordial space. In order to create the world, therefore, God first needed not to expand or reveal more of the divinity but to contract—a self-limiting that Luria called *tzimzum,* which created the space for something other than God. In this process, God "exiled" the divine self from boundless infinity to a more "concentrated infinity," as Gershom Scholem put it (*Messianic Idea,* p. 44).

Into the darkness God beamed streams of divine light: emanations spreading slowly in stages through various realms as they traveled between the heavenly and the new world. Our material world is the last, outermost shell of the garment of the deity, to use the term in the *Zohar.*

These emanations were placed into vessels, or *kelim,* which kept the divine light from reverting to the original source and which give form to the divine qualities contained in those streams—qualities necessary to the functioning of the world. In this way, divine attributes like justice and mercy, qualities made imperative by the original fall of Adam, entered the world. To the kabbalists, creation was to be a permanent Eden-like existence. Adam's sin in the Garden changed all that. People would now be in exile from perfect harmony and would need divine help to achieve redemption. These emanations, God's self-revelation, would bring divinity to the world and create the potential for righteous existence.

Unfortunately, catastrophe struck—unexpected, sudden, and devastating. The *kelim* couldn't hold the essences of God. They exploded from the intensity of the light in a process called *Shvirat HaKelim,* the shattering of the vessels. Most of the liberated light reascended to its original divine source, but some sparks remained stuck to the fragments of the shattered vessels. The sparks of divine light became trapped in these shells, or husks, each of which Luria called *kelipah.* Within each *kelipah* lived forces of evil and demonic power, according to the mystics. So, the evil and divine light, enmeshed and imprisoned together, plunged into primordial space.

The kabbalists thus found in the Ari's kabbalah a shockingly different explanation for their plight, one that was built into his conception of how the world came to be. Clearly, they knew more traditional explanations offered in the Holy Torah, which teaches that pain is punishment for sin, for violating the covenantal agreement sealed at Sinai. God brings about suffering as a consequence of human action. So traditionalists had to assume not only that what had befallen them was a legitimate consequence of their shortcomings but also that their Spanish persecutors were agents carrying out the divine will. God had exacted retribution, and they had no one to blame but themselves.

EVIL IS CAUSED BY A COSMIC ACCIDENT

The Ari begged to differ. Evil came to the world not because of something we did or as a divine response. Rather, there had been an accident. Evil was the inadvertent result of cosmic, not human, chaos. It was not possible for us to prevent what was unforeseen and unstoppable. Transcendent forces were at work, and we were their hapless victims.

But, contended Luria, people were not powerless in the face of this tragedy. In fact, there was great urgency in the air. Not only were the people of Israel in *galut*, in exile, but the *Shekhinah*, the divine presence of God, was in *galut* as well. Nothing could be right and orderly as long as God was weakened by this dispersion of the divinity through the realms of existence. Luria here universalized the experience of exile. Not only were the Israelites uprooted from their proper place in the world, but so was the entire world, all in desperate need of finding harmony.

This was stunning theology, and Luria knew it. He well understood that his ideas could stun the ear. But he was wrestling with every assumption he had made about God. Our Torah taught that God was merciful, God was just, and God loved the people of Israel deeply. But how did this core belief stand up to what had happened to the truly pious people who surrounded Luria in Safed? The only conclusion he could come to was that God was unable to act at will. God's omnipotence had been compromised in a dramatically new way. Luria doubtless understood that God willingly had ceded some control to human beings at the outset of creation. In creating us in the divine image, in giving us the ability to choose between life and death, the blessing and the curse, God had given us incredible power over our own destiny. Testing the limits of human temerity, God wanted to know how Abraham would respond to the destruction of the cities of Sodom and Gomorrah, what he would do when commanded to take his only remaining son and bind him for sacrifice.

God must have been amazed at Moses' tenacity when they stood together on Mount Sinai and witnessed the building of the golden calf. Now a broken man, Moses, so close to God, risked his own life in pleading for the life of his people. He did so by appealing to the divine ego and reminding God of the promises made to Abraham, Isaac, and Jacob that because they had passed the test of righteousness they would be ancestors of an eternal people.

Luria also knew that Job had successfully challenged the biblical assumption that all human pain had to be caused by human sin. Both Job and Luria learned that lesson "out of the whirlwind."

WE AND GOD ARE IN THIS TOGETHER

So, the Torah's accounts seemed to support the view that God had ceded some omnipotence in order for us to be potent. By choice. But Luria was not satisfied. In his interpretation of history, Luria believed that the forces of darkness were overwhelming the forces of light, that both people and God had been weakened by the shattering of the vessels. There had been no thunderbolt from heaven, no divine retribution for the wanton acts of the human species. All was now in turmoil, but now, even more than in biblical times, God and humanity truly were in this together.

Luria wasn't content simply to find the solution to the question of why bad things happen to good people. His belief in *tzimzum,* the emanations of light, and *Shvirat HaKelim* was a description of how things were in his world. All were in exile: the *Shekhinah,* the people of Israel, and the world as a whole. But— and here was the good news—they didn't have to stay there.

Luria had a great deal of faith in the divine-human relationship, and much optimism in the inherent goodness of human beings to rise to their potential in relationship to God. He believed that there is something we can do about the scattering of the divine sparks trapped within the evil matter. We can liberate these sparks in a process Luria called *tikkun,* or repair.

The world is in disorder, but we are not powerless to help. The process whereby God's light is restored to its original source was almost completed once before. Almost everything had been restored to its proper place, and the first man's pure essence made it possible for him to attach his whole being to the spiritual source and achieve the communion with God necessary for *tikkun.* But, alas, Adam failed. Adam's sin broke his communion with the higher spheres; thus, he cohered to the evil forces of the "other side." Adam's soul, which had contained all other human souls, no longer could contain them, and many souls joined the sparks of the divine trapped within the *kelipot.*

Now, it's up to us. Jewish textual history is generally consumed with what God can do for us. Luria challenges this paradigm to assert that there is much we can do for God. By carefully prescribed prayer, chants, and rituals, all infused with fervent intention, or *kavanah,* coupled with observance of the Torah and *mitzvot* done with equal precision and passion, we can repair the divine flaw. We can restore the Holy One to full power and glory and to a rightful place in the universe.

WE ARE GOD'S PARTNERS IN REPAIRING THE WORLD

By first tending to ourselves, to our own souls, we next address the next soul and the next in a process called transmigration until all humanity is engaged in the work of *tikkun*. Any one of us can be a prism for the sparks of the divine, and every one of us can be involved in what Luria called "the raising of the sparks" in what is, in effect, the healing of the divine. We are God's partners in the crucial process of repairing ourselves, the world, and ultimately God.

Luria here shows tremendous faith in human beings—at least in that strata of society spiritually attuned enough to engage in mystical activity. In fact, his followers responded enthusiastically—even arrogantly—sharing the Ari's view that we are not continual sinners constantly in need of divine reproach. Nor are we hapless victims of fate beyond our control and explanation. They too believed that there is explanation, there is control, but it's in human hands. Even today, all of us have a real responsibility to ourselves, to fellow Jews, to the rest of the world, and to God, and we dare not shirk our duty.

When life hits us over the head, we too easily retreat to the posture of the victim and ask "Why did God do this to me?" For too many people, this is a safe harbor; if God did it to me, there is nothing I can do about it except wring my hands and say "Woe is me." Luria puts forth a total theory of how the world really works, asserting that no one is doing it to anybody. Rather, we're all in this together, and we will sink or swim in concert.

Luria gives us our marching orders. In so doing, he restores to us a true sense of human dignity. Unique among living creatures, we were given the tools for an awesome responsibility and resplendent blessing: putting God back together again. In so doing, we right the course of our lives and infectiously spread righteous behavior all over the world. The result will be the redemption of humankind and the coming of the messiah.

FOR LURIA, THE MESSIAH IS A GOAL, NOT A PERSON

Notice what the messiah is for Luria. The messiah doesn't enter the abyss and liberate good from evil. That's *our* responsibility. What happened to the world did not constitute the "birth pangs of the messiah." Apocalypse was not sent to us as a messianic precondition. Chaos was a cosmic accident in need of repair—nothing more, nothing less.

In this scheme, the messiah wasn't there on the way down and won't necessarily be present on the way up. In fact, Luria makes no strong case that the messiah in fact is a person at all. For Luria, the messiah is much more an ideal symbolizing the completion of the process of *tikkun*, when the whole world will taste the fruits of redemption. On that day, God will be One again, and the world will be united in harmony. All will be back to where it should be, where it was meant to be before Adam's sin and before the breaking of the vessels.

As Gershom Scholem puts it: "The messiah himself will not bring the redemption, rather, he symbolizes the advent of redemption, the completion of the task of emendation. It is therefore not surprising that little importance is given to the human personality of the messiah in Lurianic literature, for the kabbalists had no special need of a personal messiah" (*Messianic Idea,* p. 48).

For Luria, the messiah is not a single person but is at least that segment of the entire people of Israel willing and able to do *tikkun.* Each one of us has a role. A prayer, a *mitzvah,* a kind act are no mere gestures. Done in the kabbalistically proper way, they constitute the beginning of a process of repair and thus have far-reaching, cosmic significance.

Your life can have true purpose. You are here to be a healer, not just of your own wounds and those of your loved ones but of others as well. You can heal the world and—believe it or not—God too. One *mitzvah* at a time.

For it is just possible that there is no messiah.

And you're it.

———————◆———————

10

The Worldwide Embrace of Sabbatai

L URIANIC KABBALAH couldn't be confined to Safed. Luria's doctrine spread slowly throughout the world over the next fifty years. Its impact was strongest in Italy and Poland. So popular did kabbalah become among the masses that notable rabbis, such as Moses Isserles, author of the Ashkenazic commentary to the *Shulchan Aruch,* the code of Jewish law composed by Sephardic mystic Joseph Caro, felt compelled to lash out against such "ignorance":

> Many of the unfettered crowd jump at kabbalistic studies, for they are a lust to the eyes, especially the teachings of the later masters who expounded their doctrines clearly and in detail. . . . Not only do scholars try to study it, but even ordinary householders who cannot discern between their right hand and their left hand and who walk in darkness unable to explain (even) a portion of the Pentateuch or a chapter of the same with Rashi's commentary, rush to the study of kabbalah. . .but they will have to render account (at the day of judgment) (*Sabbatai Sevi,* p. 178).

Rabbinical protests were quite ineffectual, and kabbalistic speculation spread among both eastern and western Jews of all social classes. As we discussed, Luria attempted to dampen ardor about a personal redeemer who would be sent by God to lift people from their plight. Personal responsibility was called for as sparks of the divine were to be extracted from the *kelipot*. Each individual could find within his soul the possibility for *tikkun*. You would think there would have been little temptation to embrace messianic personalities who would inspire great hope for a better life and who inevitably engendered crushing disappointment.

You would be wrong. In fact, the vast majority of the Jewish people were taken on a messianic roller coaster by a man named Sabbatai Tzvi, who, in the words of the great scholar Gershom Scholem, "was a man afflicted by the most severe mental imbalance who tottered between heights of ecstasy and depths of melancholy in steeply alternating manic-depressive stages" (*Messianic Idea,* p. 60).

How did Sabbatai Tzvi come to be so widely embraced as the messiah, particularly after such influential thinkers as Moses Maimonides and Isaac Luria had developed spiritual systems whose by-product was surely a reduction in messianic speculation? Little in Sabbatai's early biography hints at the broad-based appeal his persona would acquire.

Sabbatai was born in Smyrna in what today is called Turkey, on Tisha B'Av 1626, the second of Mordechai Tzvi's three sons. His father was a wealthy trader of commercial goods, but both his parents died before his messianic movement began. Sabbatai appeared to have a traditional Jewish education and was encouraged to pursue rabbinical studies. Somewhere along the way he appended kabbalah to his more conventional Jewish academic work, but he pursued those studies privately. Sabbatai appeared to crave a life of solitude, viewing aloneness as critical to piety.

Though he was caught up in the popularity of Lurianic kabbalah, he appeared to have distanced himself from its doctrines. He specifically abstained from the chants and meditations so critical to *tikkun* and the Lurianic system. Perhaps he had too many psychotic ego needs to be attracted to Luria's popular understanding that everyone was able and responsible to participate in *tikkun*. But whereas he may not have shared Luria's enthusiasm for personal responsibility, he had a personal magnetism that was infectious. Sabbatai was most charismatic. Even though his manic depression manifested itself in shifting exultant and depressive moods, he mitigated concern about all this with an embracing warmth and a quiet nobility that succeeded in gathering about him a growing circle of admirers and adherents.

SABBATAI, THE SELF-PROCLAIMED MESSIAH

This young rabbi, who was soft-spoken and ascetic by nature, could get away with demonstrating extraordinarily bizarre and shocking behavior during moments of public exaltation. Passing through Aleppo, Syria, in 1665, he described to Rabbi Solomon Laniado how God's voice had spoken to him, saying, "Thou art the savior of Israel, the messiah, the Son of David, the anointed of the God of Israel, and thou art destined to redeem Israel, to gather it from the four corners of the earth to Jerusalem" (*Sabbatai Sevi*, p. 136).

Traditionally, such revelations from God were met with humble protestations. The Prophets unfailingly resisted the call to their mission and begged God to choose someone else. Sabbatai's response was precisely the opposite. Despite dire warnings against pronouncing the ineffable four-letter name of God, Sabbatai began to do so and urged his followers to pronounce God's name as well—sure signs that he fully believed himself to be the messiah and hence not subject to conventional prohibitions. Later he would cast aside much of the traditional law and practice of Judaism, freely moving Sabbaths and holy days to other places on the calendar, revealing new rituals that would bring mystical perfection to all the world.

Repercussions soon followed. The Rabbis not only severely criticized him but actually flogged him as punishment for his actions. Repeatedly, he would retreat into anguish, guilt, and self-doubt, but he always returned with renewed manic gusto to flaunt his disdain of much that Judaism held dear.

Many felt that he was possessed by demons. Surely, when he was not on a "high" he wouldn't even countenance his own behavior. A note from Sabbatai's own hand was purported to say, "Thus speaketh the utter fool." It is safe to say that from his first appearance in Smyrna in 1648 until his public proclamation that he was the messiah in Gaza in 1665, not a single person would have regarded Sabbatai as the messiah.

What changed? Many scholars point to social and political conditions that were breeding grounds for messianic yearnings. Chief among them were the populist Chmielnicki massacres of 1648, led by the Cossacks against Jewish communities in Poland and the Ukraine. These attacks resulted in the destruction of three hundred Jewish communities, the death of close to one hundred thousand Jews, and the exile of countless refugees. Displaced persons arrived as far south as Turkey, where their horrifying tales became widely known. Messianic fervor typically grew in periods of such displacement and despair. Adding to speculation that such massacres were really the birth pangs of the messiah, and that these souls were liberated from the *kelipot* on the road to redemption, was a passage from the *Zohar*, the seminal mystical tract of the twelfth century, promising the final resurrection of the dead in the year 1648, coincident with the Chmielnicki massacres. "In the year 408 [1648] of the sixth millennium, they that lie in the dust will arise. . ." (*Zohar* I, 139b).

Gershom Scholem also points to economic factors that bred great insecurity. Inequity in personal wealth widened considerably in all the important population centers of Poland in the seventeenth century. While the poor were feeling increasingly vulnerable and disenfranchised, the rich were subject to the extortions and financial demands from ruling powers and the economic changes that came from wildly unpredictable political developments. In Scholem's view, this accounted for the instability shared by all social classes of the Jewish people throughout the world. Thus, all were hungry to be liberated from the cruel vicissitudes of life punctuated by ever-present anti-Semitism amidst unstable political and economic times.

But can any of this fully explain the Sabbatai Tzvi phenomenon? Political and economic uncertainty was a fact of life for European Jewry in virtually every generation. Brutal anti-Semitic attacks, too, were constant companions for Jews. External social and political factors cannot fully account for the world's embrace of a seemingly paranoid schizophrenic as messiah.

Nor can the personality of Sabbatai. Surely stories of his daringly blasphemous behavior spread far and wide. But why was he not dismissed as an unstable person who had to be stopped lest traditional Jewish authorities be undermined? Part of the answer has to lie in the power of the messianic idea, which has never lost its hold on the imagination of Jews, Christians, or Muslims. Despite historic disappointments resulting from investment in false messiahs, subsequent generations always seem to be in search for a fresh personality, someone who with a sweep of the scepter will illumine the path, reduce the pain for people everywhere, and take the burden of responsibility for social betterment—*tikkun*—away from us.

After all, didn't the prophet Malachi predict, and the Passover Seder yearly underscore, the fact that Elijah will arrive and presage the coming of the messiah? Such a powerful idea seemed much too tempting to dismiss outright. Moreover, even though messianic candidates had come and gone over the years, it had been quite a long time since a false messiah like Bar Kokhba had left the debris of utter destruction in his wake and had so affected historic memory that the community at large would never go down that road again. This anesthesia had long since worn off, and the community seemed ready to take the plunge again.

THE SELLING OF THE MESSIAH

Another factor looms large here: the power of peer pressure. Ludicrous ideas become credible if enough people talk them up and influence one another toward acceptance. Never underestimate the power of a campaign to convince people of what they never could accept on their own. Ask political operatives who sometimes start out with weak candidates and ill-defined messages. But with enough money and exposure, they can package the candidate to be sold to a susceptible public. Soapsuds are surely sold that way. So are messiahs. It just takes a great salesman—and Sabbatai was immensely fortunate to have one. His name was Abraham Nathan ben Elisha Hayyim Ashkenazi, and he became known simply as Nathan, the prophet of Gaza. Nathan's father had come to Jerusalem via Poland or Germany, so Nathan was of Ashkenazic background. Doubtless he had heard a great deal about this strange man of wildly fluctuating moods and actions, but what drew Nathan to Sabbatai was a vision that came to him soon after he began the study of kabbalah at age twenty.

Nathan described his vision in a letter he wrote in 1673:

> I was undergoing a prolonged fast in the week before the feast of Purim. Having locked myself in a separate room in holiness and purity, and reciting the penitential prayers of the morning service with many tears, the spirit came over me, my hair stood on end and my knees shook and I beheld the *merkabah* [the mystical chariot], and I saw visions of God all day long and all night, and I was vouchsafed true prophecy like any other prophet, as the voice spoke to me and began with the words: "Thus speaks the Lord." And with the utmost clarity my heart perceived toward whom my prophecy was directed [that is, toward Sabbatai Sevi], even as Maimonides has stated that the prophets perceived in their hearts the correct interpretation of

their prophecy so that they could not doubt its meaning. Until this day I never yet had so great a vision, but it remained hidden in my heart until the redeemer revealed himself in Gaza and proclaimed himself the messiah; only then did the angel permit me to proclaim what I had seen. I recognized that he was [the] true [messiah] by the signs which Isaac Luria had taught, for he [Luria] has revealed profound mysteries in the Torah and not one thing faileth of all that he has taught (*Sabbatai Sevi*, pp. 204–205).

NATHAN'S MESSIANIC PLATFORM

What is crucial about this vision is that a scholar of some repute recognized the messiah in Sabbatai. Nathan was a man of real intelligence, true passion, and tireless energy. Nathan was at once "the John the Baptist and Paul of the new messiah" (Ibid, p. 207). If Sabbatai could be characterized as being withdrawn and passive, possessing little vision and theological focus, Nathan was just the opposite. Nathan, who occasionally dreamed of a messianic calling himself but could never put himself forward with such temerity, became, therefore, a "transformer," publicly working to translate the bizarre actions of Sabbatai into a messianic platform. The first person Nathan had to convince in Gaza in 1665 was Sabbatai himself. When Nathan addressed him as the messiah, Sabbatai laughed at him and said, "I had it [the messianic vocation], but have sent it away" (Ibid, p. 215).

In fact, Sabbatai had come to Gaza not to become the messiah but as a supplicant to Nathan the prophet, the "doctor of souls," in quest of *tikkun* and peace for his tormented being. Nathan had acquired a reputation for helping people, for being a man able to read people's secrets written on their faces, and to prescribe repentance and proper *tikkun* accordingly.

Sabbatai, who was extremely troubled by the emotional roller coaster he was on, and by his inability during periods of stability to even recognize the personality who emerged during periods of ecstasy or depression, came to Gaza looking for help. Nathan must have shocked him when he said that Sabbatai's soul was "of a very high order which needed no *tikkun* and that, in fact, Sabbatai was the messiah" (Ibid, p. 215). This had to take a while to digest, but with the self-assured Nathan consistently giving him confidence, Sabbatai slowly warmed to the prospect of pronouncing himself as the messiah. This took place at a prayer service where he took the self-ascribed title *Mashiach Elohei Yaakov,* the anointed of the God of Jacob, on the seventeenth of Sivan (May 31), 1665. As he later remarked, he went to Gaza as a *shaliach* (an emissary) and returned a *mashiach* (messiah) (Ibid, p. 214).

Sabbatai took to his role almost immediately, incorporating the feeling of self-deification and appropriating for himself extraordinary leeway in normative Jewish practices. While Nathan was busy preaching traditional repentance and imposing fasts and mortifications on supplicants, Sabbatai was abolishing traditional fast days and altering liturgy.

This was enough to rile the Jewish establishment in Palestine, and rabbinic opposition to him was strong. Jerusalem's rabbis expelled him from the holy city and placed him in *herem* (excommunication). But the credibility of the prophet Nathan, who could interpret Sabbatai's idiosyncrasies to fit the messianic mold, and the hunger of the people for a redemption that would come without their having to sacrifice too much personally, together overwhelmed the opposition.

Absence also makes the heart grow fonder. As Sabbatai traveled abroad to places like Aleppo in northern Syria and Smyrna in Turkey, people in Jerusalem could focus less on the instability and unpredictability of the actual person and more on the abstract promise of the messiah they yearned for. It can't be stressed enough how crucial Nathan's passion and message were to Sabbatai's success. Not only was his endorsement critical, but his traditional call for belief, repentance, and prayer provided comforting cover to Sabbatai's flaunting of everything they had come to understand as sacred and holy.

Nathan could thus continue to champion his messianic candidate. On September 5, 1665, Nathan heard a voice from the celestial academy proclaiming that the messiah, Son of David, would become manifest to the world in a year and some months. In a letter written probably in that same month, Nathan put forth some audacious claims, which seemed to undermine Lurianic kabbalah's emphasis on individual responsibility in the *tikkun* process.

As a result of the messiah's struggle against demonic powers (an ingenious interpretation of Sabbatai's behavior), the last sparks of divine light had been liberated from their captivity in the realm of the *kelipot* or shells. So, Nathan contended, Luria's calls for meditation and *kavanot,* intense chants and prayers, were no longer necessary. Traditional kabbalah taught that at the time of redemption the full power of God's light caught up in the *sefirot* would be made manifest on earth. Now it would be triggered by the messiah himself.

Sabbatai would do more. In a little more than a year's time, Nathan predicted, Sabbatai would take dominion from the Turkish king without a war. He would discover the exact site of the altar of the yet unrebuilt Holy Temple in Jerusalem as well as the ashes of the red heifer, and would perform sacrifices there. Then he would proceed to the Sambatyon River (where, according to our tradition, tribes were often exiled and which was thought to possess magic powers) and would return "mounted on a celestial lion, his bridle will be a seven-headed serpent with fire bellowing out of his mouth" (Ibid, p. 274). Seeing this, all the nations and all the kings would bow before him, the ingathering of the exiles would take place, and the Temple would appear already built, descending from above. On that day, the resurrection of those who had been buried in Palestine would occur, with the resurrection of those outside the Holy Land happening some forty years later.

MESSIAH'S CENTRALITY TO THE PROCESS OF *TIKKUN*

Nathan suffused Lurianic kabbalah with a new emphasis: the centrality of the messiah in the process of *tikkun*. The messiah's soul was trapped deep within the *kelipot*. In bondage there since the beginning of the world, the messiah struggled amid great suffering to free himself from this trap and to achieve redemption. So, Sabbatai's strange actions were necessary for his escape from the *kelipot* and his achievement of holiness.

The messianic awakening originated in Palestine, but it was only after Sabbatai left the Holy Land, and particularly after the experiences of mass enthusiasm in Smyrna, that the movement began to mature and spread far and wide. In Smyrna, where he stayed for about four months, he was alone, without Nathan, his prophet. Then and only then did he achieve the confidence to publicly show himself to be King of the Jews. The response was wildly positive among both the wealthy merchants and the poorest people in town. Even some rabbis jumped on the bandwagon, perhaps motivated by the traditional call of the return to Zion, perhaps not wanting to get in the way of the people's rabid resolve. Carpets were spread before him lest he soil his feet. Acclaim was his (Ibid, p. 391).

The stage was set for the event that truly began his rule over the Jewish community in Smyrna and beyond. As I mentioned in chapter 7, it took place at the Portuguese Synagogue on a Sabbath day when, in response to the elders locking the door in fear of Sabbatai, he smashed the doors to the synagogue with an ax, preached a blasphemous sermon, and declared that "Today you are exempt from the duty of prayer." He then forced men and women alike to pronounce the Ineffable Name of God (Ibid, p. 397).

After reading the Torah from a book instead of a scroll, which he proclaimed to be holier than the Torah scrolls, he cupped his hands and trumpeted in all four directions in order to "comfort Satan and weaken the power of the *kelipot*" (Ibid, p. 398).

He explained his actions by saying that since it was time to work for the Lord, the law could be transgressed. When he broke down the doors of the synagogue he taught that many *kelipot* possessing evil power had thus been broken. He capped off this stunning performance by taking a Torah scroll from the ark and singing a Castilian love song: the story of a lover who lay with the emperor's beautiful daughter. He interpreted this song as an allegory of himself, who was like "a bridegroom coming out of his chamber, the husband of the beloved Torah" (Ibid, p. 400).

Sabbatai's feverish demeanor drove him from one provocative demonstration to the next. He issued royal decrees, slandered fellow Jews before the Turkish authorities, and declared that he was the King, against whom they had committed royal abuses. Furthermore, he decreed that all fasting commemorating the destruction of the Temple and Israel's exile was to be discontinued, "the sorrow of the fast turned into the rejoicing of gladness" (Ibid, p. 414).

Sabbatai certainly had his share of detractors: "unbelievers," as they were dubbed. But it was clear that Sabbatai had taken Smyrna by storm. Trade and commerce in the city came to a standstill. Banquets, processions, and dancing, interspersed with penitential activities—all prescribed by Nathan—created a festive mood of mounting exhilaration. The traditional prayer for the ruler of Turkey was supplanted and replaced by a new text:

> "He who giveth salvation unto Kings and dominion unto princes . . . may He bless, preserve, guard and exalt ever more our Lord and messiah, the Anointed of the God of Jacob, the messiah of Righteousness, the King of Kings, the Sultan Sabbatai Tzvi" (Ibid, p. 424).

EMBRACE OF THE QUIXOTIC MESSIAH

The transformation seemed complete. The vast majority of Jews in Smyrna and increasingly in other places were prepared to bow before the King of the Jews and exult in the messianic world that would emerge. The carefully plotted manner in which they had built their lives and fortunes gave way to a charismatic but shockingly unstable figure who convinced the people to believe and do the inconceivable. How could so many sophisticated, intelligent people have been led so far astray?

The idea of a messiah seems to have been so compelling that many were prepared to abandon logic and follow this quixotic personality into a messianic future. The desire for someone to come along and do what they probably could do for themselves, but chose not to do, was so strong at certain moments in Jewish history that they simply would not be deterred. Even when shocking new facts about Sabbatai came to light, his greatest admirers were quick not to reject the messiah but to change their view to accommodate the messiah they were intent on embracing.

11

The Surge to Sabbatai

S ABBATAI'S REIGN AS King of the Jews was shockingly short-lived. He was arrested by the Turkish authorities in Constantinople and kept in "the most loathsome and darkest dungeon in the town." Facing the choice between death and conversion to Islam, Sabbatai startled both his adherents and his detractors by renouncing his past, rejecting Judaism, and embracing Islam.

But Sabbatai can't be dismissed from history so easily, nor can he be written off as one of a long line of false messiahs. The Sabbatean movement was a widespread phenomenon. At least by way of warning, it is important to understand how successfully this messiah was sold and thus how difficult it was for some supporters to let go even after Sabbatai's shocking renouncing of his entire package.

MESSIANIC FERVOR

Some lines from an eyewitness letter give a sense of what was reverberating across Europe:

> First of all, there were many people everywhere who fasted the whole week and immersed themselves every day. . . . They devoted the whole day to good works, and recited the daily devotions as arranged at that time. At night men would lie

down naked in the snow, and roll in it for half an hour or at least a quarter of an hour. Then they would take thorns and nettles and scourge themselves until their bodies were covered with blisters, and every day they would take a scourging with a hard lash. . . . Some caused boiling wax to drip down their naked bodies for an hour or more, others again wrapped their naked flesh in nettles and put on heavy clothes in order to increase the mortification of the flesh. . . .

People tried to sell goods and belongings at any price they could get, and kept themselves in readiness for the moment when the messiah and the prophet Elijah would appear and announce the end, so as to be able to proceed [to the Holy Land] without delay. . . . And let no one say that I have exaggerated in my description, for you should know that what I have written is not even a half of what has been reported, by not one but by hundreds of trustworthy witnesses who have told most wondrous things of the repentance that was wrought in our parts [that is, Germany, Holland, etc.] (*Sabbatai Sevi,* pp. 473–475).

It has to be emphasized that for the first time since at least the destruction of the second Temple, the majority of the Jewish people had been united in renewed hope, energized by a man who generally manifested truly strange and sometimes morose behavior.

But this is what happened. It's safe to say that few of Sabbatai's adherents ever had a personal encounter with him, so they were caught in a contagion that acquired an unstoppable momentum.

How could that be? Why would people be so willing to lose themselves in a movement with such unstable grounding? Can peer pressure really cause us to lose all rational sensibility? Is our hold on reality really that fragile? Perhaps it can be argued that because we have been so downtrodden and oppressed, we will grasp at any promising straws to relieve us of our misery. This could be a compelling explanation, except for the fact that the communities that enjoyed the most freedom and prosperity actually took the lead in

Sabbatean renewal. Major centers of Jewish life such as Salonika, Amsterdam, and Venice fanned the flames of messianic pursuits. These were vital centers of commerce, not downtrodden outposts.

In *Sabbatai Sevi, The Mystical Messiah*, Gershom Scholem cites several reasons why this messianic movement caught on so well:

- The messianic call came from the Holy Land and thus inherently had more spiritual prestige.

- Messianic manifestations were accompanied by a renewal of more traditional prophecy. Nathan's credibility was underscored by his call for more familiar acts of repentance, which were necessary preconditions for national redemption.

- Sabbatean doctrine was a compelling mixture of traditional Jewish apocalyptic notions together with interpretations of Lurianic kabbalah, which could produce more immediate results with less burden to adherents than Luria's original doctrine. Obtaining redemption without having to do the real work of *tikkun* may have been particularly alluring to many people.

- This movement did not divide the people by region or social class. All could find what they needed in it. So there was comfort not only in numbers, but in the feeling that if conservative community leaders and even some rabbis could find this movement palatable and this messiah viable, who are we to argue? (Ibid, pp. 463–467).

While communities far and wide were preparing to change their life to embrace Sabbatai Tzvi as the messiah, Sabbatai was moving precisely in the opposite direction. Turkish authorities regarded him as someone who was fomenting rebellion, not only destabilizing Turkish society but enticing the Jewish community to slow down their economic pursuits, so central to the financial well-being of the empire. So, while accounts differ as to how it all unfolded, essentially Sabbatai was told to convert to Islam or die. Apparently, Sabbatai eagerly embraced this new faith, renounced Judaism and any messianic pretensions, and blamed Nathan of Gaza for forcing the messianic role upon him against his will.

In response, the Turkish Sultan graciously accepted the convert, permitted him to assume his new name of Mehemed Effendi, and appointed Sabbatai to the honorary office of *kapici bashi,* keeper of the palace gates. He was clothed in robes of honor and received a purse full of silver.

This new Sabbatai had thus turned on a dime. In a letter penned in his own hand, Sabbatai revealed his new action plan:

> Know ye brethren, my children, and my friends that I recognized with great clarity that the True [God] whom I alone know for many generations and for whom I have done so much, has willed that I should enter with all my heart into the Islamic religion [*din islam*], the religion of Ishmael, to permit what it permits, and to forbid what it forbids, and to nullify the Torah of Moses until the time of the End. For this is important for the glory of His Godhead and for His revelation that I should induct herein everyone whose soul would agree with me. . . (Ibid, p. 840).

Sabbatai had so captured the imagination and tapped into the need of his generation that even such shocking words from his own pen were not enough to end his messianic reign. Some followers still wanted to know, and would continue to want to know for a long time, the real hidden and covert reason for the alleged apostasy to another faith.

SABBATAI'S CONVERSION SHOCKS THE JEWISH WORLD

The shocking turn of events Sabbatai Tzvi caused by his conversion to Islam didn't quite have the impact it would have had in the present day. Today a press conference would be called, and CNN would televise Sabbatai's speech instantaneously all over the world. Reaction would be swift. In the seventeenth century, news didn't travel so quickly. Since it was spread by parties more and more at a distance from the actual event, skepticism abounded. The movement had taken on a momentum and an inner dynamic that almost defied real-time historic events. A confluence of factors, perhaps impossible to fully grasp and explain, had caught the entire Jewish world in its grip.

When adherents did absorb the news that Sabbatai had really converted to Islam, they were stunned. Jews the world over were subject to ridicule by people of other faiths and nationalities. Confusion reigned everywhere. "Believers" would have understood if he had accepted martyrdom *al kiddush haShem*—to sanctify God's name. And if Sabbatai had seized the Sultan's crown, he would have taken his rightful place on the messianic throne. But doing it the way he did brought shock, then shame, to Jews everywhere.

Reactions, though, came slowly and varied widely. Some "believers" became introspective and found it hard to believe they had been so gullible. Others felt that all this was the work of the devil. By this theory Sabbatai had begun as a holy man but couldn't resist the evil power that had gripped him. Some withdrew from the movement into a grieving process for the death of a dream. Others rationalized his behavior, refusing even now to give up believing. This newly minted Muslim was still their messiah, they persuaded themselves, but he had to disguise himself for a while in order to best fulfill his mission.

No doubt some Jews were prepared to follow Sabbatai's lead and continued to spread his message. Interestingly enough, however, this seemed to be done on a very limited basis, as no excommunications from the community (the probable punishment for such deeds) were reported for the whole next year by the Rabbis who desperately sought to ban messianic activity and regain control of the community (*Sabbatai Sevi*, p. 715).

THE "HOLY SINNER"

Nathan, still an ardent supporter, gave Sabbatai's actions an ingenious kabbalistic twist: Sabbatai had entered the realm of the *kelipot*. He had descended into Hell in order to reinvigorate that realm with the potential for holiness. Now he was, for some, a "holy sinner," and thus the movement could continue a little longer on some sort of rational basis.

While the Turkish authorities were remarkably subdued, realizing that a crackdown could fan the flames of smoldering messianic embers, the Jewish authorities soon cracked down on Sabbatai's behavior. Believers were no longer permitted organized activity or public demonstrations. Outward manifestations of Sabbatean practice—chantings, pronouncing the Ineffable Name of God, new rituals—all vanished. No one dared admit to being a "believer." Nathan, himself, who was still feared by the Rabbis, led the life of a fugitive until his death in 1680, but he never stopped believing in Sabbatai. In fact, he insisted on the necessity of the messiah's apostasy. In a private letter, here is how Nathan put it:

> The statement [in the *Zohar*] that in the last exile the [messiah's] name would become an object of scorn and derision no doubt refers to the fact that he will don the turban. . . . Yet we [the true believers] have learned that the Sabbath has not been profaned because of his donning the turban . . . but he had to act thus because of the sins of Israel, and his fate was similar to that of Esther who had to eat forbidden food [in King Ahasuerus' palace]. . . . Wherefore, my brethren and all faithful believers in Israel who stand and wait and tremble at these words, be strong and of good courage, be not affrighted nor dismayed, turn unto the Lord your God with all your heart and all your soul and give thanks unto His great name (Ibid, pp. 742–743).

Sabbatai went further than living a life within Islam. He urged his followers to convert as well, even going so far as to preach apostasy in the synagogue. Many of his followers saw this as a test of faith in Sabbatai's messianism. Ironically, there was criticism even among his followers for those who joined Sabbatai in Islam. But for core adherents of Sabbatai—a dwindling number, to be sure—Sabbatai was simply doing what he had to do to fulfill his mission.

Sabbatai and Nathan were not through with their delusion. Sabbatai finally became convinced of his own divinity. In a letter to Jews in Salonika, Nathan spoke of the messiah's ascension to "the rank of perfect Godhead" (Ibid, pp. 871–872). This belief was a perfect corollary to one of Sabbatai's only "original" contributions to the development of kabbalah. Sabbateans put forth the notion that the *Ein-Sof*, the "cause of all causes," exercises neither influence nor providence in the lower worlds. The "God of his faith" emanated from a higher principle and is the divine self, which interacts with the world (Ibid, p. 912). Though he didn't specifically discuss his own place in the spiritual hierarchy when revealing the mystery of the Godhead, this scheme seems to have given Sabbatai the place he wished to occupy in the divine realm: not the First Cause but the divinity that has contact, influence, and power in the divine and human realm.

A few months before his death in 1676, he issued one more statement underscoring his divine role: "But if thou shall indeed obey his voice and do all that I speak to you (Exodus 23:22), then I shall indeed go up and fill your treasures (Proverbs 8:21). Thus saith the man who is raised to the heights of the Father, the Celestial Lion and Celestial Stag, the Anointed of the God of Israel and Judah, Sabbatai Mehemed Sevi" (Ibid, p. 916).

ENDING SABBATAI'S MESSIANIC REIGN

Members of the Jewish community continued to speak out against Sabbatai's increasingly heretical pronouncements but were rather ineffectual in getting rid of him. After all, he enjoyed the Sultan's special protection. What could they do? Finally, they resorted to a plan to bribe a well-placed official, who orchestrated Sabbatai's arrest on the charge that he had turned Muslims into Jews. That plan failed to completely convince the authorities, but when the Sultan and his Grand Vizier paid a visit to the imprisoned Sabbatai in Adrianople, Turkey, they seemed to believe reports that Sabbatai had uttered blasphemies against Islam and had been seen "wearing phylacteries and a Jewish bonnet (instead of a turban) surrounded by women, wine and several leaders of his sect" (Ibid, p. 875). In any case, the Grand Vizier, who had been Sabbatai's protector, now believed that Sabbatai was hostile to Islam. He was therefore ready to cooperate with Jewish leaders in getting rid of the opportunistic messiah.

Sabbatai was not killed but exiled. The Turkish authorities seemed to want to keep the location of his exile secret so as to lower the emotional temperature in relation to the Jews. Since the rabbis in Turkey threatened excommunication to anyone who as much as mentioned Sabbatai's name, Turkish Jews seemed to have no first-hand knowledge of where he lived out his last days on earth.

Sabbatai did wind up in Albania, where he lived a solitary existence. He had some contact with the faithful in some communities and with Nathan. It was there that Sabbatai's doctrine of the mystery of the Godhead and his belief in his own divinity were finally articulated. Both he and Nathan seemed to become broken men at the end. Even Nathan, the ever-confident progenitor of Sabbatean messianism, seemed to fall victim to despondency. But Nathan never stopped believing. Even Sabbatai's death was one more opportunity to push the messianic envelope. While opponents used Sabbatai's death as a true vindication of their understanding that he was a fraud, Nathan espoused a new doctrine of "occultation," whereby a person, by the grace of God, is liberated from death at the very moment of death and is brought up to Paradise, where he continues to live in the same body.

With a kabbalistic twist, Nathan taught that Sabbatai had ascended to and been absorbed in the "supernal" light of the *Ein-*

Sof. Furthermore, "Our Lord [Sabbatai] had gone to our brethren, the children of Israel, the Ten Tribes, that are beyond the river Sambatyon, in order to marry the daughter of Moses. If we are worthy, he will return at once after the wedding celebration to redeem us; if not, then we will tarry there until we are visited by many tribulations" (Ibid, p. 924).

In fact, Nathan remained faithful to Sabbatai's messianism to the end of his life. This was his singular mission, and to fail to reinterpret each painful twist in the road in a way that validated his messianic dream would have been to admit that his life's work had failed and that he too had perpetuated a cruel hoax on the Jewish people. Perhaps that was more than Nathan and his core followers ever could face up to.

LOSING CONTROL TO A FALSE MESSIAH

We are still left with the stunning fact that most of the sophisticated Jewish world had an immense hunger to embrace a kabbalistic path that took responsibility and control from them and placed it completely in the hands of a man whose own needs were so profound and complex, he couldn't see beyond himself and understand the damage done to thousands of his faithful supporters by shattering their dreams.

Perhaps Nathan should have understood this better. But he was so busy promoting Sabbatai—selling the product, as it were—that he never stopped long enough to understand how shallow was Sabbatai's true resolve and what would be the implications of this for Nathan's own life and that of the Jewish people.

HARD TO ABANDON THE FALSE MESSIAH

But Nathan had done such a good selling job to a vulnerable public that there were people who refused to abandon this messiah even now. He had filled their life with excitement, purpose, and hope, and they were not prepared to give it all back. If Sabbatai had converted to Islam, he must have had a worthy reason for doing so. The messiah simply had to be understood, not abandoned. Clearly, this small group of "believers" would follow Sabbatai and his mission anywhere, even to places that Sabbatai himself never could have imagined.

12

A "Frank" Messianic Descent

YOU CAN'T HELP but be impressed by how firmly the messianic idea has held our people in its grip throughout the ages. Some impulse or need keeps forcing us back into the gravitational pull of the messiah. Even when a particular candidate spectacularly disappoints, like Bar Kokhba or now Sabbatai, there is always a group of people, albeit small and dwindling, ready not to admit failure but to look for the true motive behind the messiah's actions. What keeps these people in the movement? Why, after all is said and done, do they remain "believers"?

In my judgment, it is close to impossible ever to understand why someone believes something. So we should be careful in analyzing why the "radicals" were prepared to follow messianic figures away from normative practices even into apostasy. Their motives are probably as varied as the iconoclastic personalities who dotted the post-Sabbatai landscape. Just as Sabbatai was a product of his own schizophrenic impulse, we cannot eliminate psychological disorders as a fueling factor in the sentiments of such "believers."

WHY SOME REBEL AGAINST JUDAISM

The temptation to find understanding can get the better of all of us, even the most expert in the field. Gershom Scholem jumped into the fray with the following explanation of why some ardent believers were prepared to go to the other side: to convert out of Judaism.

> Feelings such as these formed the psychological background for the great nihilistic conflagration that was to break out in the "radical" wing of the Sabbatean Movement. The fire was fed by powerful religious emotion, but in the crucial moment these were to join forces with passions of an entirely different sort, namely, with the instinct of anarchy and lawlessness that lie deeply buried in every human soul. Traditionally Judaism had always sought to suppress such impulses, but now that they were allowed to emerge in the revolutionary exhilaration brought on by the experience of redemption and its freedom, they burst forth more violently than ever (*Messianic Idea*, p. 109).

The instincts of anarchy and lawlessness buried in every human soul? That's quite a statement! In my judgment, "believers"—even radicals—are attracted to their movements often because the tried and true normative path just isn't working. Religious traditionalism becomes commingled in their minds with political orthodoxy to produce an authority that is as oppressive as it is ineffectual. Something else is needed to address the lust for meaning, the desire to have the world make more sense than it does.

It seems to me that people act not because they look for boundless freedom from convention—the equivalent of donning a motorcycle jacket and disappearing into the sunset. Rather, they want to be able to make sense of a world that often seems adrift from its rational moorings. Having lost confidence in the stewards of authority, they want to play more of a role in the reconstituted reality that will give their lives meaning. People don't usually want to simply drift away to nihilistic pleasure.

They seek not anarchy but a commitment to something that

will make them more than rusty cogs in a barely turning wheel, that will allow them to be vital contributors to social change and redemption. Bar Kokhba offered them that, but he fell in disastrous military defeat. Lurianic kabbalah appealed to personal responsibility, but the results were slow in coming and depended on a very long chain of events for *tikkun* ever to happen.

Most "believers" retreated from Sabbatean activity, devastated that Sabbatai hadn't seized the messianic crown from Turkish authorities but had simply taken the easy way out. Yet, others were convinced that before them lay the road to the messiah. Sabbatai had actually showed them the way. If Islam was good enough for him, why should they not take the plunge as well? This was a dangerous road on which the sanctifying power of sin was celebrated and the belief was espoused that *Bittulah shel Torah zehu kiyumah:* "the violation of Torah now is its real fulfillment."

Here Sabbatai had picked up on the differentiation in the *Zohar* between the world of *atzilut,* or emanation, and the world of *beriah,* or creation. The Torah of *atzilut,* which reveals the "mystery of the Godhead" is the "true" Torah, though it has been practiced in secret. All the commandments and prohibitions of the actual Torah, the Torah of *beriah,* are to be reinterpreted by the light of the world of *atzilut.* So, for example, there no longer existed forbidden sexual practices as the progenitors of this convoluted belief embraced the holiness of sin (*Messianic Idea,* p. 110).

Some of the "radical believers" remained traditional Jews outwardly while inwardly adhering to the Torah of *atzilut.* Others followed Sabbatai into Islam. Gershom Scholem discusses the existence of a crypto-Jewish sect called the Donmeh, who outwardly converted to Islam but refused to interact or intermarry with either Muslims or Jews. Their strange orgiastic rituals were often rumored and widely reported (Ibid, pp. 142–144).

A FRANK EMERGES ON THE SCENE

Another group followed a man of considerable ambition and ego named Jacob Frank. Frank (1726–1791), born Jacob ben Judah Leib, who spent at least twenty-five years in Turkey and was thought to be a Turkish subject, actually comported himself like a Sephardic Jew and spoke Ladino in public. He was enthusiastically received by the "believers" in Eastern Europe as news spread about the appearance of a *frenk,* the usual Yiddish term for a Sephardic Jew.

Soon, Jacob assumed "Frank" as his family name. Early in 1757, he officially became a convert to Islam and was highly praised by Turkish authorities. But he was not to remain in that fold. Like early Christians, Frank apparently came to believe that the messiah was no mere human being but an incarnation of God in human form. Frank obviously felt that he had superseded Sabbatai in his work, for he believed that Sabbatai was powerless to achieve anything because he was unable to find the true "way."

"But my desire is to lead toward life," he declared. This path entailed the embrace of nihilism, freeing oneself from all conventional laws and ultimately converting to Christianity—but to a faith no devout Christian ever would recognize: "Wherever Adam trod, a city was built, but wherever I set foot, all will be destroyed, for I came into this world only to destroy and to annihilate. But what I build will last forever" (Ibid, p. 130).

Frank's daughter Eva was revered by the Frankists as the Virgin. One day she was supposed to give birth to the true messiah and form the Trinity with two other god-incarnates, the First Cause (Sabbatai) and the God of Israel (Frank). But this Virgin had many lovers, and sexual relations with her was seen as a "holy" act.

Frank prepared his followers for baptism as a final step that would open for them "the way to Esau." In his mind, this was the path that Esau's brother, Jacob, had promised to follow in the Bible (Genesis 33) but never did because the journey was too difficult. Now the time had come to travel that road, which no Jew had traveled before. It was the road upon which the Virgin would be revealed as well as the true and good God, who had been hidden and divested of any link with this world. All the great religious leaders, from the patriarchs to Sabbatai Tzvi, had tried to find the way to God but had failed (*Encyclopedia Judaica*, Vol. 7, p. 59).

This path that led to "the true life" entailed the abandoning of all law, the embrace of religious anarchy, and the assumption of *massa dumah,* or a heavy burden of silence (Isaiah 21:11). While it was necessary to inhabit the outer garb of Christianity, Frank believed that Jesus of Nazareth was no more than "the husk preceding and concealing the fruit, who was Frank himself." Ironically, Frank's messianic vision was ultimately of a Jewish future, albeit in a totally upside-down and revolutionary form. So, although he insisted on an outward demonstration of Christian fealty, he forbade his followers to mix with Christians or intermarry with them (*Messianic Idea*, pp. 130–131).

Such studied ambivalence toward changing faiths may account for the fact that some Frankists followed their leader to the baptismal font whereas others did not. Interestingly enough, "believers" in Eastern Europe were more likely to become Christian than those in western Europe. Gershom Scholem surmises that this may have been because of social caste. "Believers" in Germany and Austria were from wealthier backgrounds and had more substantial traditional Jewish learning which could have accounted for their reluctance to leave Judaism.

POST-SABBATEAN OPTIONS

The post-Sabbateans could be divided roughly into four groups, all of which represented radical departures from the Jewish community. These "believers" were divided into those who openly converted to Islam; those who outwardly adhered to Judaism but in effect rejected the Torah of *beriah* in favor of embracing the Torah of *atzilut;* Frankists who converted to Catholicism; and Frankists in places like Moravia, Hungary, and Romania, who chose to stay, at least marginally, within the Jewish fold (*Messianic Idea,* pp. 114–115).

While Frank was widely distrusted in the Jewish community, he was viewed with even more suspicion in the Christian community. His belief that he was the living incarnation of God meant that his followers' real locus of devotion was Frank, not Christ. This was more than church leaders could bear, and Frank was arrested in Warsaw on February 6, 1760.

For three weeks, he underwent intense interrogation by an ecclesiastical court. The jurists decided to exile him to the fortress of Czestochowa, which was firmly under the jurisdiction of the Church. There the Church authorities could keep their eye on him and prevent him from establishing contact with his followers. He remained in captivity there for thirteen years. Thereafter, his followers attempted to influence turbulent political affairs in Russia.

Meanwhile, his followers gained some political and economic toeholds in various communities. They were businessmen, writers, and lawyers. It is not surprising that as Frank's personal influence waned these believers were swept up into the passion of the Jewish Enlightenment *(Haskalah)* and the French Revolution while increasingly being seen in the fashionable revolutionary circles of Paris and Strasbourg.

What united them all was a disdain for conventional authority and a desire to overturn that which stifled revolutionary impulses. That some Frankists ended up transferring their inwardly focused messianic aspirations to more outward political activity is not surprising, given the tenor of the times. But it is a far cry from Scholem's exaggerated claim that these "believers"—in effect the last Sabbateans—"had been drawing closer to the spirit of the *Haskalah* (Enlightenment) all along, so that when the flame of their faith finally flickered out they soon reappeared as leaders of Reform Judaism, secular intellectuals, or simply complete and indifferent skeptics" (Ibid, p. 140).

What kind of people were willing to follow a man of such complete narcissism that he not only would risk the destruction of his ancestral faith as an ego-driven exercise but would presume to take on the mantle of God incarnate? Seemingly, they were people who were so needy and weak-willed that they would follow such a progenitor of dangerous ideas anywhere, or who were so revolutionary that they had no desire to transfer their energies even to progressive "establishment" movements.

FRANK'S DUBIOUS LEGACY

We should not wax poetic or enthusiastic about Jacob Frank and his followers. Theirs was a celebration of nihilism and self-absorption without consideration of the consequences. Ego-gratification was Frank's obsession, and it is scary that there were enough people to fuel that need without due concern for what they were doing to their people, their tradition, and their God.

The danger of following a messiah who cares little about what God wants him to do or about the desire of people to live a purposeful life, but who is consumed with the idol worship that is accomplished by looking in the mirror, should become apparent to modern Jews as well. Hopefully, the Jacob Franks of the world will teach us—perhaps scare us—to sublimate that impulse within to follow someone blindly for instant gratification and instead craft a life of meaning and purpose that will not flame out as quickly as the false messiah *du jour*.

13

Hasidism: The New Look in Messianism

F OR ALL THE EXCITEMENT they generated, the Sabbatean movement and the Frankist phenomenon were, relatively speaking, like comets: bursting onto the scene with explosive power,
but withering in short order as the key personalities driving the
movement proved to be colossal disappointments. Hasidism, on
the other hand, which was the last major movement to take hold
before the modern period, arrived on the scene with the same
quickness. Far from petering out, though, it fanned out from the
Ukraine throughout Russia and Poland, and it established an
influence over people that is keenly felt to this day.

As Dr. Art Green put it, "We would search Jewish history in
vain for another phenomenon of religious transformations that
succeeded in so rapid and yet so long-lasting a manner . . . .
Hasidism, in one or another of its forms, dominated Jewish
religious life in Russia, Poland, and parts of neighboring
Hungary and Romania throughout the nineteenth century. It
continues to play a major role in Judaism today, both through
the survival of the Hasidic communities themselves and
through its influence, however transformed, on even the most
thoroughly modern of Jewish religious thinkers" (*Back to the
Sources,* p. 361).

IS HASIDISM A MESSIANIC MOVEMENT?

Even though the success of the movement can be traced to the proliferation of communities organized around the inspired leadership of the rebbe, who was viewed as the mediator between heaven and earth, Hasidim were careful, particularly in their early years, not to proclaim any of these religious leaders, or *tzaddikim*, as the messiah. Hence, the important question for our purpose is whether this too was intended to be a messianic movement, perhaps another manifestation of Sabbateanism, or whether, in its emphasis on joyfully expressed but inner-directed piety, Hasidism can be seen as a movement to postpone or even subvert the outer-directed messianic impulse.

That is Gershom Scholem's view. He believes that kabbalah had to undergo one of three types of profound changes after the Sabbatai Tzvi calamity. One could underplay the whole phenomenon and go back to the world as it was. Second, one could renounce any widespread movement for fear of being swept along by a false messiah into catastrophic behavior. A third way, the way of Hasidism, is to keep alive kabbalistic Judaism, with its emphasis on efforts to gain real intimacy with God, but to strip away much of its messianic thrust. Thus, you would be left with all of the impulses for personal responsibility and self-satisfaction found in Lurianic kabbalah without the hypnotic and destructive lure of a Sabbatai or a Jacob Frank. In Scholem's own words:

> Hasidism represents an attempt to preserve those elements of Kabbalism which were capable of evoking a popular response, but stripped of the Messianic flavor to which they owed their chief successes during the preceding period. That seems to me the main point. Hasidism tried to eliminate the element of Messianism—with its dazzling but highly dangerous amalgamation of mysticism and the apocalyptic mood—without renouncing the popular appeal of later Kabbalism. Perhaps one would rather speak of a "neutralization" of the Messianic

element. I hope I shall not be misunderstood. I am far from sug-
gesting that the Messianic hope and belief in Messianic
redemption disappeared from the hearts of the Hasidim. That
would be utterly untrue. . . . But it is one thing to allot a niche
to the idea of redemption, and quite another to have placed
this concept with all it implies in the center of religious life and
thought. This was true of the theory of *tikkun* in the system of
Lurianism and it was equally true of the paradoxical
Messianism of the Sabbatians; there is no doubt what idea
moved them most deeply, motivated them, explained their
success. And this is precisely what Messianism had ceased
to do for the Hasidim (*Messianic Idea,* p. 180).

As authoritative as Scholem is in this area, there is much to
quarrel with in this analysis. First, whereas Sabbatai and his followers used Lurianic kabbalah and its restorative elements to
put themselves at the center of the system and, arguably, in their
neurosis and egocentricity, even to supplant God, I would not say
that the idea of one particular personal messiah was the centerpiece of Luria's vision. On the contrary, what gave the system its
real oxygen was the infectious soul-to-soul growth inherent in the
process of *tikkun. Tikkun* was born in the heart, soul, and yearning of the individual, not necessarily the messiah. In fact, without the common person's efforts to free the divine sparks from
the *kelipot,* no messianic efforts could have borne fruit. The messianic elements in the system, relatively speaking, were
appendages to this effort, not the core of the journey.

Moreover, I take issue with Scholem's contention that the
"belief in messianic redemption disappeared from the hearts of
the Hasidism." One of the most important documents in Hasidic
writing is the letter written by the founder of Hasidism, the Ba'al
Shem-Tov (Besht) to his brother-in-law, Rabbi Gershon of Kutov,
which underscores the profound connection between the Hasidic
mystical journey and messianism.

The Besht there wrote:

On Rosh ha-Shanah of the year 5507 I performed an incantation [hashba'ah] for the ascent of the soul, known to you. And in that vision I saw wondrous things, which I had never seen until then from the day that I became spiritually aware. And it is impossible to relate and to tell what I saw and learned in that ascent thither, even in private. And I asked my teacher and master that he come with me, as it is a great danger to go and ascend to the supernal worlds, whence I had never ascended since I acquired awareness, and these were mighty ascents. So I ascended degree after degree, until I entered the palace of the Messiah, which is the place that the Messiah learns Torah, together with all the Tannaites and Amoraites and the seven shepherds. And there I have seen a very great joy. . . . And I asked the Messiah: When do you come? And he answered: "You will know [the time] which is when your doctrine will be revealed in public and it will be disclosed to the world, and your fountains will well outside, what I have taught you and you apprehended, and also they [the people of Israel] will be able to perform the unifications and the ascents [of the soul] as you do, and then the shells will be abolished and there will be a time of good will and redemption." And I was surprised by this [answer] and I was deeply sorrowful because of the length of the time when this will be possible: however, from what I have learned there, the three things which are remedies and three holy names, it is easy to learn and explain. Then my mind was calmed and I thought that it is possible for my contemporaries to attain this degree and aspect by these [practices] as I do, namely to be able to accomplish the ascents of souls and they will be able to study and become like me (Idel, *Messianic Mystics,* pp. 213–214).

Scholem's answer to this letter is that it really doesn't testify to a strong messianic thrust in the Besht's outlook. On the contrary,

Scholem is saying, by assigning the coming of the messiah to a distant time, the Besht is throwing cold water on messianic impulses. Postponing the coming of the messiah does for the Besht what it did for the Rabbis of the talmudic period, who, in composing the blessings of the *Amidah* prayer unit, were actually, in some scholars' views, composing a checklist for messianic aspirants. You really think such and so is the messiah? Let's see. Has justice prevailed? Has repentance taken place? Have Jews returned to their homes and rebuilt the Temple? Setting the bar high for messianic candidates had the effect of cooling the temperature of a people in messianic heat (*Messianic Idea,* p. 185).

The Besht doesn't seem to be doing any such thing. Though at first he was saddened by the task at hand, he realized that his contemporaries could develop the spiritual awareness and study skills to accomplish the ascent of souls necessary to achieve messianic goals. This was not to happen at some distant time. It could happen now in his lifetime.

Scholem is not through. He believes that the centrality of the doctrine called *devekut,* or communion with God, is "clearly a contemplative value without messianic implications." *Devekut* is defined as the intense concentration of one's thought *(mahshavah)* and mind *(sechel)* and spirit on God to the point where one achieves not union with God, but a true communion with the Holy One.

Devekut, for Scholem, at best can accomplish salvation of soul for the individual. "But redemption of the soul without redemption of the social body, i.e. of the nation from its historical exile, of the outward world from its broken state, has never had a Messianic meaning in Judaism" (Ibid, p. 194). Scholem repudiates this spiritually focused, inner-directed messianism with this statement: "Let us accomplish our task of personal salvation, it seems to say, and forget about the messiah" (Ibid, p. 195).

THE INNER FOCUS OF HASIDIC MESSIANISM

Clearly, Scholem doesn't like this shift of direction. Like it or not, though, the focus of messianism had changed. It did turn inward. Being scorched by pogroms will do that. So will being burned by false messiahs who raise expectations to fever pitch, then summarily crash them back to earth. Since I can't trust those messianic candidates, the thinking may go, I will stay close to home, concentrate on my own *tikkun,* and focus on those leaders, those *tzaddikim* or rebbes that I can come to know personally, and thus can cohere my messianic yearnings to a more trusted source.

In localizing and internalizing the messianic mission, Hasidism reconnected with Lurianic kabbalah. By circumventing the messianic imposters who arose in the name of Lurianic kabbalah, Hasidism brought kabbalah back to its roots: individual responsibility for *tikkun,* which will lead to the redemption of the many, after which the messiah shall arrive.

If Hasidism stripped messianism of its apocalyptic, painful elements while deemphasizing the social, the political, and even the ethical role of the restorative process, it did not postpone or subvert the messianic mission. It just changed it. Perhaps it is not an exaggeration to say that Hasidism saved messianism from the dustbin of history by salvaging what it could from the Sabbatean and Frankist debacles.

Messianism's importance in Hasidism was underscored in the book of teachings by Shneur Zalman called *The Tanya.* Shneur Zalman was the founder of the now familiar, popular sect that took its name from its principal center of activity, the town of Lubavitch. In his important writings about the messiah, Shneur Zalman teaches that each Jew has a role in readying the world for the messiah. We do this by removing the "garments" that keep the impending messiah from finding a home in the world. Our bodies can be such a "garment," but by purifying ourselves through joyous observance of *mitzvot,* we can remove the material husks that keep the divine sparks imprisoned. With joyous hearts, fervent prayer, Torah learning, and obedience to God, each and every person from the most learned to the least can have a role in bringing on the *mashiach* (Arthur Hertzberg, *Jews,* p. 159).

The Tanya offers more than abstract speculation about the coming of the messiah. Shneur Zalman proclaims that the "Sabbath of the world" will come in the seventh millennium according to the Hebrew calendar. Coincidentally, his seventh-generation descendant Menachem Mendel Schneerson, the twentieth-century Lubavitcher rebbe, was virtually obsessed with the expectation that the messiah was poised to appear (Ibid, pp. 160–161).

As I said previously, most Jews are quite familiar with the Lubavitcher Hasidic movement. Their dress, lifestyle, and political influence all breed fascination and sometimes hostility among Jews and non-Jews alike. They have missionizing efforts all over the world, and their *mitzvah* mobile is seen in larger cities everywhere. Their goals seem simple and honorable enough: get Jews to do more *mitzvot.* Frequently, Lubavitchers will stop passersby (male, of course) to ask whether they have put on *tefillin* today. Next, they invite them into the van for morning prayer. Such work earns them admiration far and wide, but their simple piety masks a hard-core right-wing political agenda, both in the United States and in Israel.

MESSIANIC HUNGER IN LUBAVITCH

One of Lubavitch's core beliefs is in the coming of *mashiach.* As this book demonstrates, there is nothing new in this expectation. But Lubavitch aggressively asserts that the *mashiach* is coming NOW. In an interview published in the Lubavitch magazine *Wellsprings* (May, 1992), before the Rebbe's death, spokesman Manis Friedman told Professor Susan Handelman that the Rebbe put emphasis on the idea of *"Moshiach"* now because the miracles he had seen in recent days, such as the United States victory in the Persian Gulf War, were of far greater significance than the miracles of survival we have experienced in the previous thousands of years. To reinforce this central belief, the Lubavitchers, often known by their acronym *Chabad,* conduct a *mashiach seudah,* a messiah meal, on the final day of Passover, when they believe that the messiah's coming is imminent. In format, this is similar to the traditional Passover Seder *(Pesach Seder),* held a week earlier, but particular emphasis is placed on the coming of the messiah.

During his lifetime and after his death, speculation grew to a fever pitch about whether the Rebbe Menachem Schneerson was the messiah and whether he thought he was. The Lubavitch community at first was deeply split on the question when the Rebbe was still living. That his life pretty much fit the time frame predicted by *The Tanya* was overshadowed in importance by the fact that he was last in a dynastic line of seven Grand Rebbes of Lubavitch. The lack of male heirs and of a known successor in waiting has added to the urgency of those who believe that he properly wore the messiah's mantle.

Those in the messiah camp have unveiled publicity campaigns all over the world. A billboard in Tel Aviv has a picture of the Rebbe with the words *Baruch Ha-Ba Melech Ha-Moshiach:* "Welcome King Messiah." "Once the Rebbe told people not to sing that song, King Moshiach," noted Rabbi Yonah Avtzon, back in January 1993. "He said he would walk out. But now he has accepted the role of *mashiach.* I am convinced of that one hundred percent" (*New York Times,* January 29, 1993).

Rabbi Leibel Groner, who was a member of the Rebbe's secretariat and worked for Schneerson beginning in 1949, disagrees:

How can we say that the Rebbe is *moshiach* when the Rebbe himself told me a few months before his stroke, "How can I be *moshiach* when the *moshiach* will only be *moshiach* when God reveals him? And God hasn't told me I'm *moshiach* yet" (*NY Jewish Week,* January 22–28, 1993).

IS THE LUBAVITCHER REBBE THE MESSIAH?

Professor Arthur Hertzberg weighs in on this crucial question in the Lubavitch community:

Did the Lubavitcher rebbe, Menachem Mendel Schneerson, think that he might be the incarnation of the Messiah? I can only wonder why he would not visit the Holy Land. He never made that journey from Brooklyn, but I think not for the reason that was usually given publicly—that if he arrived there, he would be bound by the ancient rabbinic ruling that one should never leave its sacred soil. I am inclined instead to accept the whispered, deeply Hasidic reason: the seventh Lubavitcher rebbe, like the Baal Shem Tov and Nachman of Bratzlav, could not encounter the Holy Land unless it was the moment of the revelation of the Messiah, and Menachem Mendel Schneerson knew "that the time was not ripe." So he remained in Brooklyn. He even allowed his disciples to build a replica of his synagogue and headquarters in their community in Israel, a home that would be familiar to the rebbe when he did arrive in the Holy Land as the Messiah or, at least, as his precursor. Menachem Mendel Schneerson hoped that this generation could be made worthy of the coming of the Messiah, and his Hasidim kept asking out loud, Is there a more worthy candidate than our rebbe? The fires that were lit in Eastern Europe over two centuries ago by the first Hasidim still burn for some Jews everywhere in the world (*Jews,* pp. 161–2).

You might assume that those messianic fires were doused when Rabbi Schneerson died in 1994. But many of those who believed that the Lubavitcher rebbe was the messiah before his death still did not abandon their passionately held position. They posited a "Second Coming" in which he would return to complete the redemption of the Jewish people in his role of *mashiach*.

This view provoked a pained and furious response by Orthodox scholar David Berger, who in his book *The Rebbe, The Messiah and the Scandal of Orthodox Indifference* was incredulous to learn that the majority of *Chabad* would abandon the traditional criteria for the confident identification of the messiah such as the universal recognition of the God of Israel, the rebuilding of the Temple, and peace and prosperity. Berger, in turn, motivated the Orthodox Rabbinical Council of America in 1996 to declare that "there is not and never has been a place in Judaism for the belief that Messiah, Son of David, will begin his messianic career only to experience death, burial and resurrection before completing it" (p. 91).

Branding such people as idolaters, Berger courageously declared, "Lubavitch Hasidim as a group have lost their *hezkas kashrus* (presumption of being good Jews). The majority have turned the movement into a movement of false messianism" (pp. 96–97).

Dr. Berger may be rhetorically overreacting here, but he knows, as do we, the true dangers inherent in following a false messiah. Once again, in my view, the search for that one messianic persona remains elusive and futile.

As widely as we cast the net in search of a messiah out there, ultimately we will want to pull the net back and focus on ourselves as the ultimate progenitor, the vital beginning to a messianic time that we still await but that is not possible without our efforts, our passion, our vision for a Jewish future for the world around and beyond us.

It won't happen without us, because in my judgment, we will never get that final moment of absolute perfection. It will always remain an important but not fully attainable goal. But we were put on this earth to help God move the world toward justice, peace, and redemption, to make all we know better than it was because we have done our part as God's anointed ones.

Contrary to the view of many Lubavitchers today, we don't have to await the second coming of the messiah.

You are already here.

14

The Golem

THE INNER FOCUS of the Hasidic movement constituted its adherents' attempt to provide more than an intensely uplifting spiritual experience. It was also an attempt to exert some control over the seemingly uncontrollable. For many centuries, Jews have looked upward and outward for help to confront external enemies. We have never stopped praying to God as a source of redemption, but often we have not found the divine help we have sought. The search for the messiah is part of this often desperate quest to break out of the quagmires we have often felt powerless to escape. Hasidism thus came to the view that if we could not control the outer world, we could control our response to it and limit our purview to the narrowly parochial spiritual search for our own relationship with God.

Most other Jews, in this premodern era as in other times in our history, were not satisfied to withdraw from the world and focus only on our own concerns. We still wanted to feel empowered, to beat back those who wanted to consign us to the dustbin of history, and to make this a more just world. No wonder that the legend of the golem could spark the imagination of more than a few members of the Jewish people.

ORIGIN OF THE GOLEM

The golem was generally seen as a creature, usually human in form, decidedly made by human hands through magical or mystical means, with immense powers that at times escaped the control of its creators. The origins of the legend of the golem are fascinating if not entirely clear-cut.

There is only one reference to the golem in the entire Bible: Psalm 139:16, in which the term connotes flesh that is unshaped, quite without form. This reference may have been the basis for the Talmud's understanding that in the first hour of his creation, the first man Adam's dust was gathered, and in the second hour it was kneaded into a golem, into a shapeless mass (*Sanhedrin* 38b). Interestingly, even when still in the form of a golem, Adam was shown by God "every generation and its sages, every generation and its judges, scribes, interpreters and leaders" (*Genesis Rabbah* 24:2). So, there does seem to be some power of discernment and ability to shape the world even in the earliest concept of the golem.

The Talmud also records a strong hint of the magical power the kabbalists believe are inherent in certain combinations of Hebrew letters found in the Torah (which later was used to construct the golem). God commanded the angel Gabriel to set the letter *tav* in ink upon the foreheads of the righteous to protect them from the destroying angels. A *tav* of blood upon the forehead of the wicked gives destroying angels power over them (Talmud, *Shabbat* 55a). Rabbinic sage Resh Lakish said that the letter *tav* is "the end of the seal of the Holy One, blessed be He," while for Rabbi Hanina "the seal of the Holy One blessed be He, are the letters spelling the word *emeth* or truth" (Ibid).

The idea that those letter combinations possess the ability even to create creatures with impressive powers primarily comes from the mystical tract *Sefer Yezirah*, which is generally thought to have been written between the third and sixth centuries in Palestine. *Sefer Yezirah* posits the view that the twenty-two letters variously interconnected are the foundations of the creation of the world, as God "engraved upon the primal air these letters" (*Encyclopedia Judaica*, Vol. 16, p. 783). The universe is built, say the kabbalists, on the prime elements of letters and numbers because "the letters of God's language reflected in human language are nothing but concentrations of His creative energy" (*Messianic Idea,* p. 337). Every created thing contains these linguistic elements formed by the letters and exists by this power, whose foundation is God.

The Talmud also posits the notion that a person can create life, a forerunner to the stories of humans fashioning a golem. In Tractate *Sanhedrin,* "Rabbi said: If the righteous desired it, they could (by living a life of absolute purity) . . . be creators. . . . Rabbah created a man and sent him to R. Zera. R. Zera spoke to him but received no answer. Thereupon Zera said unto him: 'Thou are a creature of the magicians. Return to thy dust'" (*Sanhedrin* 65b).

THE LEGEND OF THE GOLEM

The golem becomes an actual figure among the *Hasidei Ashkenaz,* a circle of German Jewish pietists, beginning in the twelfth and thirteenth centuries. Such legends, which became widespread by the seventeenth century shared two common features: (1) These creations came to life by putting the proper combination of letters on the golem's person. In some versions of the story, the word *emet* as the "seed of the Holy One" is written on his forehead, thus empowering the golem, and when the letter *alef* is erased from *emet* it forms the world *met,* death, whereby the golem's power is eradicated. (2) The golem is the servant of his creator but develops dangerous natural powers, like superhuman strength and sight, which overwhelm other humans if not controlled by removing or erasing the right letters.

The best known of these popular legends is attributed to Rabbi Judah Loew ben Bezalel of Prague, known as the *Maharal.* Though some scholars quarrel with attributing the tale to the *Maharal,* this citing has been underscored by several authorities, including Gershom Scholem, who tells the tale this way:

Once upon a time there was a great rabbi in Prague. His name was Rabbi Judah Loew ben Bezalel and he is known in Jewish tradition as the Maharal of Prague. A famous scholar and mystic, he is credited by Jewish popular tradition with the creation of a Golem—a creature produced by the magical power of man and taking on human shape. Rabbi Loew's robot was made of clay and given a sort of life by being infused with the concentrated power of the rabbi's mind. This great human power is, however, nothing but a reflection of God's own creative power, and therefore, after having gone through all the necessary procedures in building his Golem, the rabbi finally put a slip of paper into its mouth with the mystical and ineffable Name of God written on it. So long as this seal remained in his mouth, the Golem was alive—if you can call such a state alive. . . .

All this went very well for a time. . . . One Friday afternoon, however, Rabbi Loew forgot to remove the Name from the Golem's mouth and went to the Great Synagogue of Prague to pray with the community and to receive the Sabbath. The day had barely drawn to a close and the people were getting ready for the ushering in of the holy day, when the Golem began to get restive. He grew in stature and, like one mad, began tearing about in the Ghetto, threatening to destroy everything. The people did not know how to stop him from running amok. A report of the panic soon reached the "Altneuschul" where Rabbi Loew was praying. The rabbi rushed out into the street to confront his own creature which seemed to have outgrown him and become a destructive power on its own. With a last effort he stretched out his arm and tore the Holy Name out of the Golem's mouth, whereupon the Golem fell to the ground and turned into a mass of lifeless clay (*Messianic Idea in Judaism*, pp. 335–336).

A similar telling comes to us from seventeenth-century Germany:

> After saying certain prayers and holding certain fast days, they make the figure of man from clay. . . . And although the image itself cannot speak, it understands what is said to it and commanded; among the Polish Jews it does all kinds of housework, but is not allowed to leave the house. On the forehead of the image, they write: *emeth,* that is, truth. But an image of this kind grows each day; though very small at first, it ends by becoming larger than all those in the house. In order to take away his strength, which ultimately becomes a threat to all those in the house, they quickly erase the first letter *aleph* from the word *emeth* on his forehead, so that there remains only the word *meth,* that is dead. When this is done, the golem collapses and dissolves into clay or mud that he was. . . . They say that a *baal shem* [Faith healer] in Poland, by the name of Rabbi Elias, made a golem who became so large that the rabbi could no longer reach his forehead to erase the letter *e.* He thought up a trick, namely that the golem, being his servant, should remove his boots, supposing that when the golem bent over, he would erase the letters. And so it happened, but when the golem became mud again, his whole weight fell on the rabbi, who was sitting on the bench, and crushed him (Cantor, *The Jewish Experience,* p. 120).

From thirteenth-century Spain comes a recipe for making a golem:

> Then take a bowl full of pure water and a small spoon, fill it with earth—but he must know the exact weight of the earth before he stirs it and also the exact measurement of the spoon which he is to measure [but this information is not imparted in writing]. When he has filled it, he should scatter it and slowly blow it over the water. While beginning to blow

the first spoonful of earth, he should utter a consonant of the Name in a loud voice and pronounce it in a single breath, until he can blow no longer. While he is doing this, his face should be turned downward. And so, beginning with the combinations that constitute the parts of the head, he should form all the members in a definite order, until a figure emerges (*Ibid*, translated by Gershom Scholem).

It is easy to understand why Jews would respond to the legend of the golem. No more would they have to passively wait for redemption to come from above and beyond. The golem is here, in our midst, accessible, ready for action. Nor would we have to adapt our yearnings to a message brought by some outside messianic figure. This artificial golem is made by our human intelligence and can be instructed or programmed to utilize its power to achieve our end, to be subject to our control.

GOLEM AS METAPHOR

But in these literary versions as well as in the plays based on this story, such as Leivick Halpern's Yiddish classic, *The Golem*, published in 1921, written by a man in pain from the suffering unleashed by the Russian Revolution and yearning to unleash powerful forces to combat injustice, the golem also could exercise power beyond human control and become a destructive force in its own right. As time went on, the golem was also used as a metaphor for any force created by humankind that possesses a strong and unpredictable potency. Such golems could help us celebrate our capacity to strike back against our enemies, to make sure we have the capacity to create weapons of self-defense. But they have made us aware as well of what we are producing, concerned that the solution isn't worse than the problem or doesn't create problems in its own right.

Author Isaac Bashevis Singer, winner of the Nobel Prize, considered the dangers of the golem in connection with modern technology. On the occasion of the performance of *The Golem* at the New York Shakespearean Festival, Singer wrote, "I am not exaggerating when I say that the golem story appears less obsolete today than it seemed one hundred years ago. What are computers and robots of our time if not golems?"

He went on to use the golem as a metaphor for the nuclear arms race: "While we attempt to surpass our enemies and create new and more destructive golems, the awful possibility is lurking that they may develop a volition of their own, become spiteful, treacherous, mad golems" (*New York Times*, Sunday, April 7, 2002).

DID THE GOLEM INSPIRE SUPERMAN?

A possible spin-off of the golem idea was created by two Jewish high school students from Cleveland's East Side, Jerry Siegel and Joe Shuster. In June 1938, their idea for Superman made its first appearance in *Action Comics*. The model for Superman was the dapper actor Douglas Fairbanks, Sr., but the models for the bespectacled, buttoned-up Clark Kent were none other than Jerry and Joe themselves.

Superman seemed to be an ideal messianic character. He was born on the planet Krypton but was raised from infancy by the Kent family, who found him after his spaceship had landed on earth in a cornfield. Soon, Clark discovered his miraculous powers, his ability to fly, his superhuman strength, his x-ray vision—powers that he vowed to his dying father to use only for the good of humankind and the deliverance of the oppressed. As we know, he came to stand for Truth, Justice and the American Way—which coincides quite nicely and not coincidentally with the Jewish Way.

In the novel based on the comic strip written in 1942 by George Lowther, Superman's Kryptonic name was revealed to be *Kol-El*. *El* in Hebrew means "God," and *Kol* in Hebrew means "all." Perhaps the name implies that Superman is all that God is, or at least possesses that kind of power (*Moment*, Vol. 13, No. 4). *Kol-El* also may be translated "the voice of God."

That image also beautifully fits the role I am advocating for you as messiah, God's anointed partner.

Is Superman a twentieth-century golem? I don't know whether Siegel and Shuster knew the myth of the golem, though it is highly likely they did. For one thing, the word *emet*, truth, is inscribed on the golem's forehead, perhaps as a foreshadowing of "Truth, Justice, and the American Way." Other similarities exist, to be sure. For example, the golem was supposed to defeat the enemy while obeying the will of the creator. There are differences, too. From the start, the golem's size terrifies those he is supposed to protect. In the end, the human creator can't control his creation, and the golem attacks the very people he is created to defend.

In a way, the golem became another in a line of false messiahs, the product of those who created their myths but ultimately could not control them. Certainly we could say this for Rabbi Akiba concerning Bar Kokhba and for Nathan concerning Sabbatai Tzvi. Their "messianic reign" took directions that their "creators" or sponsors could not have foreseen; the results were tragic for the population they were coming to save. Such is the danger of turning to external forces to help us and hoping they will do for us what we could probably do better for ourselves. Once unleashed, this power can't be controlled, and we are left worse off than where we started.

Superman had none of these flaws. He was always available— assuming, of course, he could find a nearby phone booth. He was all-powerful if you made sure there was no kryptonite nearby. And he was a powerful force for good. There was absolutely no downside to this messianic force for salvation. Superman was too good to be true because he was just that: too good to be true.

With him around, you didn't have to yearn for God's redemption. You didn't have to wonder when the messiah would come to help deliver us from pain and oppression.

You simply had to look up in the sky and ask: "Is it a bird? Is it a plane? No, it's Superman." And, after the show was over, he too would not help you do what you were capable of doing for yourself.

15

Introducing the Universal Messiah

T HERE IS NO WAY to overestimate the empowering effects of the Enlightenment on European society in general and on the Jewish community especially, particularly in the West. One particularly keen academic observer of social and cultural transformation, Dr. Jacob Katz, noted that at the beginning of this period, the decade of 1760–1770, Jews were regarded as no more than a part of a dispersed Jewish nation. By 1860, a Jew clearly was a fully participating citizen of France, England, and Germany, who in addition was a Jew (Introduction, *Out of the Ghetto*).

Though this newly won status was not attained instantaneously and was achieved in fits and starts, nonetheless it represented a huge substantive change in how Jews were regarded and also in how they viewed themselves. As emancipated people they now could decide whether and how fully to participate in Jewish life. No longer subject to Jewish communal sanctions for noninvolvement, they even could convert to Christianity, though instances of such documented conversions were rather rare. Moreover, they could express their Jewish affiliation in secular and political terms, not solely religious terms. This was fertile soil for the modern movements of Reform, Orthodox, and Conservative Judaism soon to be born.

One of the ironies of this newly acquired status was that

with all of the social and political freedom they now enjoyed, Jews had yet another reason to be fearful of their neighbors. With such proximity and contact on many levels, Jews didn't want to be embarrassed by their beliefs, worship style, or historic associations.

So, whereas virtually the entire world was swept up in the Sabbatean movement, believing that Sabbatai Tzvi was the messiah, now anyone even remotely connected to the false messiah was subject to attack from the organized Jewish community. Jonathan Eiberschutz, the rabbi of Hamburg, was accused of upholding the Sabbatean doctrine. Far from asserting his prerogatives to believe anything he chose in the modern era, Eiberschutz flatly denied the accusation and interpreted his own suspect writings in a way that undermined any historical association. Moses Hayim Luzzatto, a spiritual leader in Padua, was regarded by his followers as the incarnation of the messiah. Rather than being accepted as one in a line of messianic aspirants, Luzzatto was apprehended in Frankfurt on the way to Amsterdam and was sentenced in a rabbinical court to "keep a strict silence on mystical matters" (*Out of the Ghetto*, pp. 24–25).

It seems, then, that as the Jewish community expanded its horizons in the community at large, it tailored the transformation of Jewish society to what seemed acceptable—gentile even—to their new neighbors. Embrace of personal messiahs, particularly those who would lead the community on mystical flights of fancy or certainly those who would lead them back to the Promised Land, thus calling into question their loyalty to the state in which they finally were citizens, was now beyond the pale of acceptance.

Gershom Scholem has argued that the origins of Jewish enlightenment and the reforming elements in Judaism lay in Sabbatean movements and has pointed to some reformers who can trace their movement's roots back into the kabbalistic community.

But there certainly was not a straight line of descent. The

Jewish community now clearly wanted to show its bona fides to the world at large. Its Judaism was to be rational, aesthetically pleasing, and in conformity with expressed or unexpressed concerns about loyalty to the state. No movement steeped in kabbalah or even in Zionism, which would carry either the body or the soul back to Israel, could gain these reformers' support.

MESSIANIC MOVEMENT PREPARED THE GROUND FOR REFORM

What can be said is that the Sabbatean movement prepared the ground in a certain way for reform. As Professor Michael Meyer notes, in light of battles fought between Sabbateans and anti-Sabbateans in the eighteenth century, "A community so divided was less able to oppose new ideas in its midst or to project the image of unified authority that might have suppressed emergent centrifugal forces. Moreover, as anti-nomian phenomena, figures like Sabbatai and Jacob Frank helped to ensure that Jewish law was no longer unchallenged as the bond uniting all Jews. It was therefore more vulnerable to a program of reform" (*Response to Modernity, A History of the Reform Movement in Judaism*, p. 11).

In those heady days, when previously unimaginable participation in German society was becoming a reality, inevitable questions about the continued relevance of the messianic idea in Judaism came rushing to the fore. Jews had always anticipated a future that helped recapture the past. This entailed the ingathering of the exiles, the rebuilding of the Temple and life in the land of Israel, and the triumph of our one God over the forces of evil and injustice. Having now attained unprecedented status in Germany, did Jews really still want to harbor hopes of a return to Zion?

In a declaration of principles from the *Society of the Friends of Reform*, Frankfort 1842, representatives of the "radical" wing of the nascent Reform Movement explicitly rejected this core messianic belief. The third plank of the *Frankfort Platform* reads: "A messiah who is to lead the Israelites back to the land of Palestine is neither expected nor desired by us; we know no fatherland except that to which we belong by birth or citizenship" (Plaut, *The Rise of Reform Judaism*, p. 50).

MESSIANIC MOVEMENT BECAME UNIVERSALISTIC

Though this platform was attacked by both traditionalists and more mainstream reformers on several fronts, this changing view of the messiah was already achieving widespread agreement. At the rabbinical conference held in the same city of Frankfurt in 1845, the brilliant Reform leader Abraham Geiger asserted that "It shall be stated at the very outset that the loyalty to the state of even those who hold the traditional view on the messiah in its strident form is not to be questioned for a moment. The only object the conference had in view was to satisfy the demand that nothing be uttered in the prayers which contradicts present Jewish conviction" (David Philipson, *The Reform Movement in Judaism*, p. 174).

Rabbi Leopold Stein pleaded for the retention of prayers for the messianic rebuilding of Jerusalem and the Temple, believing that when the Kingdom of God will be established on earth, the holy city will arise and a holy Temple rebuilt as "the visible symbol of that spiritual brotherhood and union." But even he argued that any prayerful petition for a return to Palestine must be excised. "We know but one fatherland, that in which we live; we cannot pray 'mayest thou take us back in joy to *our* land' as though our present home were strange to us and our true home lay a thousand miles distant" (Ibid, p. 179). The concluding report of this rabbinical conference thus read: "The Messianic idea is to occupy a prominent place in the liturgy also in the future, but all politico-national elements are to be eliminated" (Ibid).

Strikingly, this view was held by much of the neo-Orthodox movement as well. Samson Raphael Hirsch, Western Ortho- doxy's most seminal nineteenth-century figure, wrote in his *Nineteen Letters on Judaism*, "Land and soil were never (Israel's) bond of union, but rather the common task set by Torah." Return to Zion was in God's hands. Though he never supported remov- ing Zionistic impulses from the prayer book, Hirsch clearly viewed the return to Zion as a pious, futuristic hope, and Jews were "prohibited from accelerating its advent." The "mission" of Israel was to disseminate "pure humanity among the nations" (*Response to Modernity*, p. 78).

Not only did the political context of messianic hopes shift sig- nificantly, so did their focus. They were universalized to an unprecedented degree. The messiah's advent would benefit not just the Jewish community but the entire world. Thus, Rabbi Moses Gutmann could assert "that far from being a particularis- tic doctrine whereby the messiah would redeem only Israel," we base our hope on the sayings of the prophets in which the mes- siah is assigned a "greater, nobler role, namely, the salvation and redemption of all mankind, the union of all nations into one peaceful realm, to serve the one true God" (*Rise of Reform Judaism*, p. 143).

Another intriguing debate ran through these conference inter- changes. With these new universalized messianic hopes, were we looking for a personal redeemer or an age of messianic redemp- tion? On this point, some lively debate took place. Stein again was in the minority that argued for a messianic personality:

> Although our hopes are for the coming of the Messianic Era of peace and good will, still we may surely leave to God the man- ner of the fulfillment; all great events in the world's history have been accomplished by great personalities; may we not then confidently expect that the greatest and highest consumma- tion of all, the ushering in of religious harmony, peace and

brotherhood will be accomplished through one sent of God? (*Reform Movement in Judaism*, p. 179).

HUNGER FOR MESSIANIC ERA, NOT A PERSONALITY

Stein, however, was in the minority of those Reform rabbis gathered for that memorable conference in Frankfurt in 1845. What was emerging in the Enlightenment period was a newfound regard for the status of the individual, the sense that each of us could do so much to effect the shared goals of harmony and social well-being. Yearning for a personal redeemer could be seen as a repudiation of the gains of stature made by and for individual Jews. Jews in the modern world don't need someone to do what we can do for ourselves, what we must do, to fulfill that special "mission of Israel," to be a light unto the nations.

Though some would argue that only God could usher in the messianic era, the idea that Israel had a mission was too strong to deny us a role in human redemption. As Rabbi Samuel Holdheim puts it: "It is the messianic task of Israel to make the pure knowledge of God and the pure law of morality of Judaism the common possession and blessing of all the peoples of the earth" (*Rise of Reform Judaism*, p. 138).

Of course, yearning for Zion certainly didn't disappear from Jewish life. It remained a strong passion for many Jews of faith, particularly in the East, and awaited the full unfolding of the modern secular Zionist movement led by Theodore Herzl and others—a movement that Jacob Katz called the "secularization of messianism." But most religious leaders of Germany, especially Reform rabbis, remained totally loyal to their new state and were unwilling to return to the passivity often associated with the wait for the anointing of the messiah.

Reformers in America continued and even furthered these trends. Here there was no state religion, no government control over worship, not even a conservative established church to set a standard for communal religious life.

The United States provided the proper intellectual climate to continue the classical Reform trends, which had planted roots in Europe such as rationalism stripped of mystical and "superstitious" ideas. Even Isaac Mayer Wise, who envisioned a single American Judaism for the new frontier and whose prayer book *Minhag America* (1857) had the look and feel of a traditional *siddur,* was still a thoroughgoing rationalist who objected strongly to those prayers "which abounded in superstitious ideas and practices."

In his *Reminiscences,* Wise reflected on his principles concerning the messiah:

> It was out of the question to return to the old prayers unchanged, because the belief in the coming of a personal messiah descended from the House of David had disappeared from among the people. The return to Palestine, the restoration of the Davidic dynasty, of the sacrificial cult, and the accompanying priestly caste, were neither articles of faith nor commandments of Judaism. The cabalistic portions which had crept into the prayer book, and the obstinate adherence to the doctrine of bodily resurrection were regarded as unjustified (Ellenson, *Between Tradition and Culture,* pp. 181–182).

So, for example, in the *Amidah* prayer, *Minhag America,* like most subsequent Reform prayer books, changed the phrase "God brings forth a personal redeemer *(goel)* for the children of their children" to "God brings forth redemption *(geulah).* . . ." Wise also rewrote all the middle benedictions of the daily *Amidah* that expressed hopes for a national restoration in the Land of Israel to reflect a more universalistic outlook.

In his more radical *Olat Tamid* (1858), a prayer book that opened from left to right and contained much less Hebrew and fewer traditional liturgical rubrics than did *Minhag America,* David

Einhorn did not change the word *goel* (redeemer) to *geulah* (redemption) on the Hebrew side of the *Amidah*. Here he followed most of the European Reform liturgies, which retained the language of a personal redeemer in the original. Make no mistake about Einhorn's intentions, though. He was not awaiting a personal redeemer sent from above. His intentions were most manifest when, in the *Yaaleah v'Yavo* prayer, he changed the phrase *v'Zichron mashiach ben David avdecha* "and the memory of the messiah, Son of David, your servant" to *v'Zichron Kol Amecha beit Yisrael meshihecha,* "and the memory of the *entire of people of Israel, your messiah.*"

PEOPLE ISRAEL ARE THE MESSIAH

Here Einhorn reveals his passionate belief that the entire people of Israel are God's messiah, brought to these shores for a redemptive mission. We are to be the carriers of God's message to the world, a light to the nations (Ibid, p. 193).

Leaders of Reform Judaism in the middle of the nineteenth century declared themselves unanimously opposed to retaining the belief in a personal messiah and the political restoration of Israel, either in their doctrine or in their liturgy. They accentuated all the more strongly Israel's hopes for a messianic age, a time of universal knowledge of God and love of humanity, intimately interwoven with the religious mission of the Jewish people. Reflecting their interpretation of the suffering servant of the Lord passages in Deuteronomy and Isaiah, they transferred the title of messiah to the Jewish nation as a whole. Reform Judaism thus adopted the belief that Israel, the suffering messiah of the centuries, shall at the end of the days become the triumphant messiah of all the nations.

While the universality of the messianic idea was reflected in an important statement of principles called the *Pittsburgh Platform* in 1885, on the hundredth anniversary of the Union of

American Hebrew Congregations and the Hebrew Union College-Jewish Institute of Religion (HUC–JIR), the centenary principles of 1976 sought to balance the mission of our people between the universal and the particular. Clearly, the horror of the Holocaust coupled with the heady promise of the State of Israel made the hopes of nineteenth-century Reform leaders seem naïve. Here's how those leaders, guided by Professor Eugene Borowitz, put it:

> The Jewish people in its unique way of life validates its own worth while working toward the fulfillment of its messianic expectations. Until the recent past, our obligation to the Jewish people and to all humanity seemed congruent. At times now these two imperatives appear to conflict. . . . A universal concern for humanity unaccompanied by a devotion to our particular people is self-destructive; a passion for our people without involvement in humankind contradicts what the prophets have meant for us. Judaism calls us simultaneously to universal and particular obligations (*Response to Modernity*, pp. 393–394).

OUR MESSIANIC MISSION

We have lived through terrible tragedy. Yet, our people have always refused to despair. The survivors of the Holocaust refused to go away and managed to show the world that the human spirit is indomitable. The State of Israel, established and maintained by the Jewish will to live, demonstrated what a united people can accomplish in history. The continued survival of the Jews alone is an argument against despair, a warrant for human hope.

We remain God's witness that history is not meaningless. With God's help we affirm that people are not powerless to affect their destiny.

While other religious movements in Judaism traditionally seemed less inclined to manifest such a clear-cut change of focus regarding the messiah, there certainly seems to be much less speculation about and yearning for a personal redeemer today—except, of course, among some sects in the Hasidic world.

In my judgment, there are two compelling reasons for this. First, because Lubavitcher Hasidim spend so much time and money talking about the messiah, their narrowly drawn views seem to co-opt discussions on these matters. But this picture of a theocratic state, a rebuilt Temple, and the reintroduction of the sacrificial cult, which can happen only when the messiah comes, fails to inspire and often alarms the vast majority of world Jewry—not to mention the political and military catastrophe that would accompany trying to rebuild the Temple where two major mosques now sit in East Jerusalem.

Furthermore, in contemplating the amount of pain and persecution our people have suffered, coupled with the disappointment felt when false messiahs have only exacerbated our sense of powerlessness, I can only conclude that God needs our help to bring redemption to our world. The Enlightenment did indeed give us a newly empowered view of ourselves. Seemingly, that is what God was waiting for: true partners who readily could use the gifts bestowed on them by their very creation. Why yearn for a messiah when you can do messianic tasks yourself?

Perhaps God never intended to send us one specific messianic individual but was simply waiting for us to recognize and embrace the messianic mission intended for each one of us—to embody the noblest values of Jewish tradition, thereby making the world the paradigm of justice and freedom God always intended it to be.

16

Our Messianic Role

HAVING MADE MY WAY through the vast amounts of material concerning the messiah in Jewish tradition, I am stunned by the tenacity of the messianic ideal in Judaism. Perhaps I shouldn't be, because the idea of the messiah seems to be part and parcel of our remarkable capacity to survive in the face of repeated and sustained attempts to consign the Jewish people to the dustbin of history.

Of course, we have not merely survived. When we had every reason to retreat and hide, to find a corner of darkness so the world would forget about us and stop tormenting us, we insisted on being a light to the nations, an affirmation of those values expected of a people living Torah: personal and political freedom, social justice, and human dignity. It's ironic that our enemies through the years have consistently sought to marginalize us, to make us invisible in the hope that we would disappear, and, failing that, to exile or exterminate us. But we have not only refused the invitation to exit the world but have insisted on participating as fully as possible in making the world a more civil and decent place—even for those who would torment us.

JEWS REFUSE TO DISAPPEAR

Having emerged from the most blood-soaked century in the history of humanity—187 million people killed, one third of the total Jewish population, two thirds of European Jews wiped out by Nazi state-sponsored genocide—you might think we would give up already and accept the fact that the Enlightenment's promise that we were finally part of the fabric of civil society and would be accorded the dignity of citizens was nothing more than a cruel illusion decimated by Nazi savagery. We emerged, in the words of the late Rabbi Alex Schindler, as debris on the banks of history. Debris usually just drifts away, but we didn't disappear, for several important reasons.

First and foremost, the world's shame that they were too indifferent to the Holocaust was the kindling necessary to reinvigorate the Zionist dream, the two-thousand-year-old hope that one day we would return to our homeland. The miracle that was the reestablishment of Israel was unprecedented in human history. Never has a civilization been destroyed and returned to reconstitute itself in another era. Israel represented the concrete promise that beleaguered Jews could have a true home where their loyalty and their right to stay alive would not be questioned.

Israel fulfilled another of the Zionist Movement's yearnings: to have a present tense. For two thousand years, Jews had to swivel their heads between the past and the future. Every time we said Kaddish or sat around a Seder table, we sanctified memory. We remembered that we were in Egypt; we stood at Sinai and joined our people's pilgrimage to the Promised Land.

We looked forward, too. For example, reading the weekly *haftorah*, we were inspired as the prophets urged us to look forward to the time when we would return to the homeland, replant vineyards, rebuild our Temple and our very lives.

Now, finally we could also live for today. Our people came back to Israel to build and to be rebuilt, to enjoy all the benefits and to confront all the problems of being a modern, democratic Jewish State.

IS ISRAEL PROOF OF THE MESSIAH?

There are those who might say that the birth of the State of Israel, the incredible military victory won in 1948 over the Arab legions who united to destroy the fledgling state and the victories that followed in 1956, 1967, and 1973, were all the proof needed to proclaim that the messiah had come. The return to Israel, the ingathering of the exiles, and the building of a strong, secure state was all Jews ever dared hope for.

Of course, there are some Jews, mostly in various Hasidic sects, who didn't greet the Jewish State as the answer to our prayers. For example, although Chabad is a tremendously active and major political player in Israel, the Rebbe, as we noted in chapter 13, ultimately never even visited the Holy Land. Though religious Zionists in a prayer for the welfare of the Jewish State called Israel *reshit tzmichat geulateynu,* the first flower of our redemption, the Satmar rebbe, in fact, views Israel as a major obstacle to redemption and insists that the messiah will never arrive as long as the modern State of Israel exists. Religious Zionism for him is nothing more than false messianism, and, in service to messianic hopes, he and his followers feel justified in taking out ads in the *New York Times* and joining the PLO in virulent attacks on the Jewish State.

On the surface, at least, many Christian evangelicals hold the precisely opposite view. Sometimes calling themselves Christian Zionists, they are a potent force in support of Israel and, in fact, do visit Israel in impressive numbers even in perilous times. It is easy to understand why some American Jews and Israelis appreciate this outpouring, but it comes with a huge asterisk. For these fundamentalists, the return of Jews to Israel and our firm political control there is a central prelude to the Second Coming of Jesus. This will be preceded by a cataclysmic messianic Battle of Armageddon, in which two-thirds of Israeli Jews will die and the rest will stay alive only to accept Jesus as messiah.

So, we should ask ourselves whether their current loyalty should be so warmly embraced, knowing as we do that their eschatological vision essentially anticipates our disappearance from the Middle East and human history as Jews. Personally, I do not trust such conditional "love."

MESSIANISM LIVES TODAY

We don't have to look to religious extremes to see messianism alive in the modern era. For instance, many German Jews in the nineteenth and early twentieth centuries were not Zionists because they believed that their messianic aspirations were totally fulfilled in the German Fatherland. America was viewed as the *goldene medina,* the Golden Land, as the United States has been described in messianic terms by Jews and non-Jews alike since the inception of the Republic. But it is Israel—the fruition of thousands of years of yearning for a return to Zion, a modern political, spiritual, and military miracle—which is most often seen as the vehicle and goal of our redemptive efforts.

For many Zionist thinkers, messianism was no longer the yearning for a specific individual but a national vision of home-coming and well-being. For the most part, Israel has succeeded beyond its founders' fondest hopes.

Today's Israel is a phenomenon, a true stable democracy surrounded by feudal Arab states and totalitarian Islamic regimes that support and harbor terrorists. Because of the success of Israel, Jews all over the world feel prouder to be Jews. Because history has clearly demonstrated that Jews share a common fate, the thriving of Israel has enhanced the self-image of Jews the world over.

TOUGH TO BE A MESSIANIC STATE

As crucial as the rebirth of Israel has been for the body and soul of the people of Israel, it is tough to live up to a messianic standard.

Now that Israel is a vibrant political entity once again, a host of challenges remain. First, Israelis have known not a single day of peace in her entire history. I write this chapter sitting in Jerusalem amidst a terribly unsettling amount of terrorist violence both in the territories and inside the so-called green line, the borders established after the 1967 Six-Day War. Today, Tel Aviv residents are afraid to visit Jerusalem, and Jerusalemites no longer travel to the Galilee through the Jordan Valley for fear of snipers. Not only are Israelis afraid to travel city to city, they think twice about going downtown, to the movies and the mall. Parents worry every time their kids leave the house. Whenever a terrorist bomb explodes, anywhere, cell phones light up with anxious relatives and friends needing to know if they are alright—this time. Visiting Israel always has been an important pilgrimage, as it was a guaranteed way to build Jewish identity for Jews of all ages. Now, tourists are greeted as heroes in Israel, as Jews here and all over the world wonder why you would want to put yourself in harm's way by visiting the Jewish homeland.

Another problem with Israel as the culmination of our messianic dreams is that this all takes into account Jewish aspirations but not those of others who live in the neighborhood. Many right-wing settlers who believe that they cannot give up one inch of land to achieve a peace agreement do not, in my judgment, live up to Jewish ideals embodied in the age-old Jewish quest for redemption. For part and parcel of the prophet's vision was that *Tzion b'mishpat Tipadeh* (Isaiah 1:27) "Zion will be redeemed in justice." Coming home meant being able to create a Jewish State that embodied the highest ideals of Torah Judaism. The Jewish ethical tradition, introduced to be sure in the Bible but fully fleshed out in rabbinic Judaism and in the Talmud and Midrash, was an ethic of the powerless. We were in exile; our hands were not on the levers of power. We were not insiders, leaders of a sovereign state, but were on the outside looking in and could afford the luxury of expecting people who were in positions of authority to do the right thing.

Now that Jews are back in power, do we pass our own test of Jewish ethics? It should go without saying that we need to defend ourselves, to be a secure people in a secure state. There is no question that many Arabs and Palestinians don't want to live side by side but would like to destroy Israel if they could. With anti-Semitism still alive around our world, there are others as well who would like to see us disappear. But we will never let that happen. Moreover, Israel is strong enough militarily and we are secure enough to struggle with the Jewish character of the State. How should we treat fellow citizens who are Arabs? Aren't they entitled to equal rights and opportunities? Can Jews who are reminded thirty-six times in the Torah that we were *gerim*, strangers, in the Land of Israel turn around and treat others as outcasts? Should Jews who drink these lessons with the four cups of wine on *Pesach* ultimately want Israel to rule over a people who chafe at our "occupation" and yearn for a similar homeland for the Palestinian people?

Leonard Fein has put our situation well:

> There are two kinds of Jews in the world.
>
> There is the kind of Jew who detests war and violence, who believes that fighting is not "the Jewish way," who willingly accepts that Jews have their own and higher standards of behavior. And not just that we have them, but that those standards are our lifeblood, are what we are about.
>
> And there is the kind of Jew who thinks we have been passive long enough, who is convinced that it is time for us to strike back at our enemies, to reject once and for all the role of victim, who willingly accepts that Jews cannot afford to depend on favors, that we must be tough and strong.
>
> And the trouble is, most of us are both kinds of Jew (*Moment*, Vol. 7, No. 8).

The bifurcated Jewish soul knows that we haven't reached our full potential as Jews in a Jewish State, that even as the only democracy in the Middle East with a strong emphasis on justice and peace, Israel can do better. So the idea of the messiah is not fully embodied in Israel—or anywhere else yet, for that matter. But we must not despair. To bring forth the messiah, we simply need to know where to look and what to do.

WHERE TO LOOK FOR THE MESSIAH

The four-thousand-year-old journey of the Jewish people has taken us to every corner of the globe. We have gone there sometimes in search of new horizons, sometimes because we had no choice. We went and we stayed and we dreamed dreams. The messianic dream often presumed the return of the Jewish people to the Jewish homeland, but it was also about creating a different kind of society right then and there, exactly where we lived. The export of Lurianic kabbalah, Sabbateanism, and Hasidism transported the messianic ideal all over the world. The Enlightenment universalized a vision that had been particularistic and Zionistic but now became a blueprint of social justice and human dignity for the world which had so newly embraced Jews as participants.

Universal messianic ideals might have found fertile ground in America, the cradle of democracy and freedom. Since World War II, particularly, American Jews have constituted the largest, most financially successful, probably the most secure Jewish community in the history of all the Jewish people. Here we have benefited from the rights and prerogatives offered to all citizens. Here, having no mother church to establish religious norms, and enjoying the separation of church and state, Jews could fully embrace their religious heritage and American birthright without equivocation or conflict. In fact, we could become deeply involved in the political process and in the battle for civil rights, equal rights, and gay rights as legitimate expressions of Torah-learned Jewish values. America, it could be argued, is as good as it gets for us—downright messianic, perhaps.

AMERICA IS NOT THE MESSIANIC DREAM

But America doesn't fully live up to the messianic ideal, either. The thousands of people who are hungry and homeless, who fall between the cracks and perhaps through the holes in the safety net, testify to the fact that we have not yet arrived. Public education rarely provides the opportunity its proponents envisioned, and justice is rarely blind to color or economic disparity.

Jews, too, have been so blessed that many fail to heed Moses' heartfelt warning that when you enter the Promised Land and have eaten your fill and have built goodly houses and raised up your flocks and your silver and gold have multiplied, you will say in your heart, "My power and the might of my hand has gotten me this wealth." The Hasidim have a wonderful expression that I mentioned earlier: There's no room for God in people who are too full of themselves.

There's no room for the messiah there, either. While it is no sin and in fact a great blessing to be successful, when even more material success becomes your life's goal, your narcissism may not permit you to see into and beyond yourself, to realize all there is still to do out there and how much potential you have to really do it.

As Rabbi Arthur Waskow put it in his book *Godwrestling*, "The most deadly danger facing the Jewish people right now is not the danger of messianic idolatry—the danger of putting so much energy into the struggle for messianic change that it begins to idolize some ephemeral approach or institution which it creates in the process of opening the way to the Days of Messiah. The most deadly danger facing the Jewish people right now is the idolatry of the status quo" (*Godwrestling*, p. 190).

Making it in America, being successful here, is a real accomplishment. In many ways we've never had it so good. But for many of us, if we are honest with ourselves, it's just not enough. There's something gnawing at us: the feeling that life is supposed to be about more than just doing well, making a good living. It's about making a good life, one we can be proud of, one our loved ones can be proud of. We should be able to look in the mirror and like whom we see. September 11 wrenched us away from the petty and mundane and forced us to ask ourselves about ourselves, our priorities, our journey, our mission.

For Jews, this has always been our quest from the very beginning of covenanted time. Four thousand years ago, God promised Abraham that we would be an eternal people. But we were expected to do much more than survive: "And I will make thee a great people and all the families of the earth shall be blessed through you. And you shall be a blessing" (Genesis 12:2).

These promises have penetrated to our very core. This is what Jews have worked and yearned for, the fleshing out of what is arguably Judaism's most compelling idea: the coming of the messiah. In my view, the messianic era is not about a brave new world preceded by apocalyptic terror. It's not about sublimating our dreams to those suffering from Bar Kokhba syndrome or paranoid schizophrenia Sabbatai style and following their vision for lack of our own. As messiah figures have come and gone and false messianism continues to rear its dangerous head, we realize that no one is going to come along and hand us truth, justice, and the American way. We get that only in comics and in the movies, not in the real world.

The real world is a messy, complicated place, where there are many hard questions, no easy answers, and lots of work to do. But inside of all of us is the capacity to live up to the potential given to us as human beings created in God's image.

The idea of the messiah has stayed alive for thousands of years because there burns within the Jewish soul the desire to do *tikkun*—to find the passion within to rescue ourselves from the *kelipot,* the husks that seduce us to be cruel, indifferent, and uncaring. When we liberate ourselves from these shackles that chain us to the status quo, we transform ourselves. Our energy, our *kavanah,* is infectious. Little by little, *tikkun* spreads soul to soul, person to person. Thus, we not only live lives we are proud of, but also make the world a better place, bring the dream of redemption closer, and even help make God all God can be by restoring the divine sparks to their original source.

ONLY YOU CAN BRING ON THE MESSIAH

We can make the messianic happen, and we can start in many different ways. We can acquire new Jewish skills that will make us feel like insiders, feel that Jewish tradition is being reborn within us. This wonderful learning adventure fuels the passion to reconnect with our history and secure our destiny. When we learn to read the Hebrew language, we feel that we are full and direct participants in the ongoing Jewish story. Prayer takes on a new meaning. So do Shabbat and the Passover Seder. When we learn how to put the *yad,* the Torah pointer, into that ancient scroll and read from Torah text, we beam ourselves back to the time when we were liberated from Egypt and stood at Sinai. We feel with ever-deepening conviction that we were there, because, in an even more profound way, we really were.

When we visit Israel and invest time, money, and love in this modern miracle, the repository of two thousand years of hope and anticipated renewal, we earn the right to insist that our homeland live up to its ideals as a true Jewish State.

When you try on new *mitzvot*—giving *tzedakah,* setting a fixed time for study of Torah, making Shabbat—you bring the world one step closer to redemption. Similarly, you can stay overnight at the synagogue's homeless shelter, become involved in a soup kitchen or in literacy programs, visit the sick, shop for the homebound before Shabbat, honor your parent(s) with the love you show when you devote real time to them.

This is messianic behavior. Some of it you are doing already. Just intensify your activity. Do it with special feeling, with *kavanah.*

You can start anywhere, because starting anywhere can lead everywhere. The Torah's special insight is that there is no bifurcation between the ritual and the ethical. Meaningful Jewish behavior entails both. Start somewhere, and you will get somewhere else. It's all mutually reinforcing. It's all messianic activity.

Do it as if your life depends on it. It may.

Do it as if the world depends on it, on you, because it does.

Arthur Waskow teaches that "it is no novelty in Jewish tradition to say that Messianic time is not the end of human history, but the beginning of a history in which God's image in humanity would be fully effective and apparent" (*Godwrestling,* p. 190).

Don't wait for some other messiah to show up to make this happen. She is already here, he is already here, to make God's image in humanity manifest for all to see.

There's no messiah—and you're it.

And from all you've discovered about yourself and will discover about the person you may yet become, it is clear that you are well worth the wait.

Suggestions for Further Reading

BOOKS

Avi-Yonah, Michael. *In the Days of Rome and Byzantium*. Jerusalem: Mossad Bialik, 1972.

Berger, David. *The Rebbe, The Messiah and the Scandal of Orthodox Indifference*. Oxford: Littman Library of Jewish Civilization, 2001.

Cantor, Norman F. *The Jewish Experience*. New York: HarperCollins, 1996.

Cassius, Dio. *Roman History*. Translated by E. Carry. Cambridge: Loeb Classical Library, 1969.

Ellenson, David. *Tradition in Transition*. Lanham: University Press of America, 1989.

Encyclopedia Judaica. Edited by Professor Cecil Roth. Jerusalem: Keter Publishing, 1972.

Enslin, Morton Scott. *The Prophet from Nazareth*. New York: Schocken Books, 1968.

Frankl, Viktor E. *Man's Search for Meaning*. New York: Washington Square Press, 1959.

Harkabi, Yehoshafat. *The Bar Kokhba Syndrome*. Chappaqua: Rossel Books, 1983.

Hartman, David. *Joy and Responsibility*. Jerusalem: Ben-Zvi-Posner Publishers, 1978.

Hertzberg, Arthur. *Jews*. San Francisco: HarperSanFrancisco, 1998.

Idel, Moshe. *Messianic Mystics*. New Haven: Yale University Press, 1998.

Katz, Jacob. *Out of the Ghetto*. Cambridge: Harvard University Press, 1973.

Kushner, Harold. *When All You've Ever Wanted Isn't Enough*. New York: Summit Books, 1986.

Maimonides, Moses. *The Guide of the Perplexed*. Excerpted in *A Maimonides Reader*. Edited by Isadore Twersky. New York: Behrman House, 1972.

Hoffman, Lawrence A., ed. *My People's Prayer Book Vol. II, The Amidah*. Woodstock: Jewish Lights Publishing, 1998.

Philipson, David. *The Reform Movement in Judaism*. New York: KTAV, 1967.

Plaut, W. Gunther. *The Rise of Reform Judaism*. New York: World Union for Progressive Judaism, 1963.

Scholem, Gershom. *The Messianic Idea in Judaism*. New York: Schocken Books, 1971.

Scholem, Gershom. *Sabbatai Sevi, The Mystical Messiah*. Princeton: Bollingen Series XCIII, Princeton University Press, 1973.

Viorst, Judith. *Imperfect Control*. New York: Simon and Schuster, 1998.

Waskow, Arthur I. *Godwrestling*. New York: Schocken Books, 1978.

ARTICLES

Green, Arthur. "Teachings of the Hasidic Masters." In *Back to the Sources*, edited by Barry W. Holtz, 361–401. New York: Summit Books, 1984.

Schulweis, Harold. "Infarct: 'Who's to Blame?'" *Moment*, Vol. 6, No. 10 (November 1981), 46–48.

About JEWISH LIGHTS Publishing

People of all faiths and backgrounds yearn for books that attract, engage, educate, and spiritually inspire.

Our principal goal is to stimulate thought and help all people learn about who the Jewish People are, where they come from, and what the future can be made to hold. While people of our diverse Jewish heritage are the primary audience, our books speak to people in the Christian world as well and will broaden their understanding of Judaism and the roots of their own faith.

We bring to you authors who are at the forefront of spiritual thought and experience. While each has something different to say, they all say it in a voice that you can hear.

Our books are designed to welcome you and then to engage, stimulate, and inspire. We judge our success not only by whether or not our books are beautiful and commercially successful, but by whether or not they make a difference in your life.

We at Jewish Lights take great care to produce beautiful books that present meaningful spiritual content in a form that reflects the art of making high quality books. Therefore, we want to acknowledge those who contributed to the production of this book.

Stuart M. Matlins, Publisher

PRODUCTION
Sara Dismukes, Tim Holtz,
Martha McKinney & Bridgett Taylor

EDITORIAL
Rebecca Castellano, Amanda Dupuis, Polly Short Mahoney,
Lauren Seidman & Emily Wichland

TYPESETTING
Kristin Goble, PerfecType, Nashville, Tennessee

COVER / TEXT PRINTING & BINDING
Lake Book, Melrose Park, Illinois

    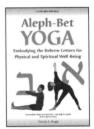

The Way Into... Series

A major multi-volume series to be completed over the next several years, ***The Way Into...* provides an accessible and usable "guided tour" of the Jewish faith, its people, its history and beliefs—in total, an introduction to Judaism for adults that will enable them to understand and interact with sacred texts.**

Each volume is written by a major modern scholar and teacher, and is organized around an important concept of Judaism.

The Way Into... will enable all readers to achieve a real sense of Jewish cultural literacy through guided study. Available volumes:

   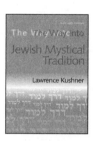

The Way Into Torah
by *Dr. Norman J. Cohen*

What is "Torah"? What are the different approaches to studying Torah? What are the different levels of understanding Torah? For whom is study intended? Explores the origins and development of Torah, why it should be studied and how to do it. An easy-to-use, easy-to-understand introduction to an ancient subject.
6 x 9, 176 pp, HC, ISBN 1-58023-028-8 **$21.95**

The Way Into Jewish Prayer
by *Dr. Lawrence A. Hoffman*

Explores the reasons for and the ways of Jewish prayer. Opens the door to 3,000 years of the Jewish way to God by making available all you need to feel at home in Jewish worship. Provides basic definitions of the terms you need to know as well as thoughtful analysis of the depth that lies beneath Jewish prayer.
6 x 9, 224 pp, HC, ISBN 1-58023-027-X **$21.95**

The Way Into Encountering God in Judaism
by *Dr. Neil Gillman*

Explains how Jews have encountered God throughout history—and today—by exploring the many metaphors for God in Jewish tradition. Explores the Jewish tradition's passionate but also conflicting ways of relating to God as Creator, relational partner, and a force in history and nature.
6 x 9, 240 pp, HC, ISBN 1-58023-025-3 **$21.95**

The Way Into Jewish Mystical Tradition
by *Rabbi Lawrence Kushner*

Explains the principles of Jewish mystical thinking, their religious and spiritual significance, and how they relate to our lives. A book that allows us to experience and understand the Jewish mystical approach to our place in the world.
6 x 9, 224 pp, HC, ISBN 1-58023-029-6 **$21.95**

Life Cycle/Grief/Divorce

Divorce Is a Mitzvah: *A Practical Guide to Finding Wholeness and Holiness When Your Marriage Dies*
by *Rabbi Perry Netter;*
Afterword—"Afterwards: New Jewish Divorce Rituals"—by *Rabbi Laura Geller*

What does Judaism tell you about divorce? This first-of-its-kind handbook provides practical wisdom from biblical and rabbinic teachings and modern psychological research, as well as information and strength from a Jewish perspective for those experiencing the challenging life-transition of divorce. 6 x 9, 224 pp, Quality PB, ISBN 1-58023-172-1 **$16.95**

Against the Dying of the Light
A Parent's Story of Love, Loss and Hope
by *Leonard Fein*

The sudden death of a child. A personal tragedy beyond description. Rage and despair deeper than sorrow. What can come from it? Raw wisdom and defiant hope. In this unusual exploration of heartbreak and healing, Fein chronicles the sudden death of his 30-year-old daughter and reveals what the progression of grief can teach each one of us.
5½ x 8½, 176 pp, HC, ISBN 1-58023-110-1 **$19.95**

Mourning & Mitzvah, 2nd Ed.: *A Guided Journal for Walking the Mourner's Path through Grief to Healing* with *Over 60 Guided Exercises*
by *Anne Brener, L.C.S.W.*

For those who mourn a death, for those who would help them, for those who face a loss of any kind, Brener teaches us the power and strength available to us in the fully experienced mourning process. Revised and expanded. 7½ x 9, 304 pp, Quality PB, ISBN 1-58023-113-6 **$19.95**

Grief in Our Seasons: *A Mourner's Kaddish Companion*
by *Rabbi Kerry M. Olitzky*

A wise and inspiring selection of sacred Jewish writings and a simple, powerful ancient ritual for mourners to read each day, to help hold the memory of their loved ones in their hearts. Offers a comforting, step-by-step daily link to saying Kaddish.
4½ x 6½, 448 pp, Quality PB, ISBN 1-879045-55-9 **$15.95**

   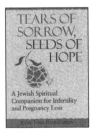 

Tears of Sorrow, Seeds of Hope
A Jewish Spiritual Companion for Infertility and Pregnancy Loss
by Rabbi Nina Beth Cardin   6 x 9, 192 pp, HC, ISBN 1-58023-017-2 **$19.95**

A Time to Mourn, A Time to Comfort
A Guide to Jewish Bereavement and Comfort
by Dr. Ron Wolfson   7 x 9, 336 pp, Quality PB, ISBN 1-879045-96-6 **$18.95**

When a Grandparent Dies
A Kid's Own Remembering Workbook for Dealing with Shiva and the Year Beyond
by Nechama Liss-Levinson, Ph.D.
8 x 10, 48 pp, HC, Illus., 2-color text, ISBN 1-879045-44-3 **$15.95**   **For ages 7–13**

Healing/Wellness/Recovery

Jewish Paths toward Healing and Wholeness
A Personal Guide to Dealing with Suffering
by *Rabbi Kerry M. Olitzky*; Foreword by *Debbie Friedman*

Why me? Why do we suffer? How can we heal? Grounded in personal experience with illness and Jewish spiritual traditions, this book provides healing rituals, psalms and prayers that help readers initiate a dialogue with God, to guide them along the complicated path of healing and wholeness. 6 x 9, 192 pp, Quality PB, ISBN 1-58023-068-7 **$15.95**

Healing of Soul, Healing of Body
Spiritual Leaders Unfold the Strength & Solace in Psalms
Ed. by *Rabbi Simkha Y. Weintraub, CSW*, for The National Center for Jewish Healing

For those who are facing illness and those who care for them. Inspiring commentaries on ten psalms for healing by eminent spiritual leaders reflecting all Jewish movements make the power of the psalms accessible to all.
6 x 9, 128 pp, Quality PB, Illus., 2-color text, ISBN 1-879045-31-1 **$14.95**

Jewish Pastoral Care
A Practical Handbook from Traditional and Contemporary Sources
Ed. by *Rabbi Dayle A. Friedman*

Gives today's Jewish pastoral counselors practical guidelines based in the Jewish tradition.
6 x 9, 464 pp, HC, ISBN 1-58023-078-4 **$35.00**

Twelve Jewish Steps to Recovery: *A Personal Guide to Turning from Alcoholism & Other Addictions . . . Drugs, Food, Gambling, Sex . . .* by Rabbi Kerry M. Olitzky & Stuart A. Copans, M.D. Preface by Abraham J. Twerski, M.D.; "Getting Help" by JACS Foundation 6 x 9, 144 pp, Quality PB, ISBN 1-879045-09-5 **$13.95**

One Hundred Blessings Every Day: *Daily Twelve Step Recovery Affirmations, Exercises for Personal Growth & Renewal Reflecting Seasons of the Jewish Year* by Rabbi Kerry M. Olitzky 4½ x 6½, 432 pp, Quality PB, ISBN 1-879045-30-3 **$14.95**

Recovery from Codependence: *A Jewish Twelve Steps Guide to Healing Your Soul* by Rabbi Kerry M. Olitzky 6 x 9, 160 pp, Quality PB, ISBN 1-879045-32-X **$13.95**

Renewed Each Day: *Daily Twelve Step Recovery Meditations Based on the Bible* by Rabbi Kerry M. Olitzky & Aaron Z. *Vol. I: Genesis & Exodus*; *Vol. II: Leviticus, Numbers and Deuteronomy*
Vol. I: 6 x 9, 224 pp, Quality PB, ISBN 1-879045-12-5 **$14.95**
Vol. II: 6 x 9, 280 pp, Quality PB, ISBN 1-879045-13-3 **$14.95**

Theology/Philosophy

Love and Terror in the God Encounter
The Theological Legacy of Rabbi Joseph B. Soloveitchik
by Dr. David Hartman

Renowned scholar David Hartman explores the sometimes surprising intersection of Soloveitchik's rootedness in halakhic tradition with his genuine responsiveness to modern Western theology. An engaging look at one of the most important Jewish thinkers of the twentieth century.
6 x 9, 240 pp, HC, ISBN 1-58023-112-8 **$25.00**

These Are the Words: *A Vocabulary of Jewish Spiritual Life*
by Arthur Green

What are the most essential ideas, concepts and terms that an educated person needs to know about Judaism? From *Adonai* (My Lord) to *zekhut* (merit), this enlightening and entertaining journey through Judaism teaches us the 149 core Hebrew words that constitute the basic vocabulary of Jewish spiritual life. 6 x 9, 304 pp, Quality PB, ISBN 1-58023-107-1 **$18.95**

Broken Tablets: *Restoring the Ten Commandments and Ourselves*
Ed. by *Rabbi Rachel S. Mikva*; Intro. by *Rabbi Lawrence Kushner* AWARD WINNER!

Twelve outstanding spiritual leaders each share profound and personal thoughts about these biblical commands and why they have such a special hold on us.
6 x 9, 192 pp, Quality PB, ISBN 1-58023-158-6 **$16.95**; HC, ISBN 1-58023-066-0 **$21.95**

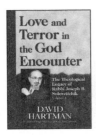    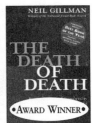

A Heart of Many Rooms: *Celebrating the Many Voices within Judaism* AWARD WINNER!
by Dr. David Hartman 6 x 9, 352 pp, Quality PB, ISBN 1-58023-156-X **$19.95**;
HC, ISBN 1-58023-048-2 **$24.95**

A Living Covenant: *The Innovative Spirit in Traditional Judaism* AWARD WINNER!
by Dr. David Hartman 6 x 9, 368 pp, Quality PB, ISBN 1-58023-011-3 **$18.95**

Evolving Halakhah: *A Progressive Approach to Traditional Jewish Law*
by Rabbi Dr. Moshe Zemer 6 x 9, 480 pp, HC, ISBN 1-58023-002-4 **$40.00**

The Death of Death: *Resurrection and Immortality in Jewish Thought* AWARD WINNER!
by Dr. Neil Gillman 6 x 9, 336 pp, Quality PB, ISBN 1-58023-081-4 **$18.95**

The Last Trial: *On the Legends and Lore of the Command to Abraham to Offer Isaac as a Sacrifice* by Shalom Spiegel 6 x 9, 208 pp, Quality PB, ISBN 1-879045-29-X **$17.95**

Tormented Master: *The Life and Spiritual Quest of Rabbi Nahman of Bratslav*
by Dr. Arthur Green 6 x 9, 416 pp, Quality PB, ISBN 1-879045-11-7 **$18.95**

The Earth Is the Lord's: *The Inner World of the Jew in Eastern Europe*
by Abraham Joshua Heschel 5½ x 8, 128 pp, Quality PB, ISBN 1-879045-42-7 **$14.95**

A Passion for Truth: *Despair and Hope in Hasidism* by Abraham Joshua Heschel
5½ x 8, 352 pp, Quality PB, ISBN 1-879045-41-9 **$18.95**

Your Word Is Fire: *The Hasidic Masters on Contemplative Prayer* Ed. by Dr. Arthur Green and Dr. Barry W. Holtz 6 x 9, 160 pp, Quality PB, ISBN 1-879045-25-7 **$15.95**

Life Cycle & Holidays

The Jewish Family Fun Book: *Holiday Projects, Everyday Activities, and Travel Ideas with Jewish Themes*
by *Danielle Dardashti* & *Roni Sarig*; Illustrated by *Avi Katz*

With almost 100 easy-to-do activities to re-invigorate age-old Jewish customs and make them fun for the whole family, this complete sourcebook details activities for fun at home and away from home, including meaningful everyday and holiday crafts, recipes, travel guides, enriching entertainment and much, much more. Illustrated.
6 x 9, 288 pp, Quality PB, Illus., ISBN 1-58023-171-3 **$18.95**

The Book of Jewish Sacred Practices
CLAL's Guide to Everyday & Holiday Rituals & Blessings
Ed. by *Rabbi Irwin Kula* & *Vanessa L. Ochs, Ph.D.*

A meditation, blessing, profound Jewish teaching, and ritual for more than one hundred everyday events and holidays. 6 x 9, 368 pp, Quality PB, ISBN 1-58023-152-7 **$18.95**

Celebrating Your New Jewish Daughter: *Creating Jewish Ways to Welcome Baby Girls into the Covenant—New and Traditional Ceremonies*
by Debra Nussbaum Cohen; Foreword by Rabbi Sandy Eisenberg Sasso
6 x 9, 272 pp, Quality PB, ISBN 1-58023-090-3 **$18.95**

The New Jewish Baby Book AWARD WINNER!
Names, Ceremonies & Customs—A Guide for Today's Families
by Anita Diamant 6 x 9, 336 pp, Quality PB, ISBN 1-879045-28-1 **$18.95**

Parenting As a Spiritual Journey
Deepening Ordinary & Extraordinary Events into Sacred Occasions
by Rabbi Nancy Fuchs-Kreimer 6 x 9, 224 pp, Quality PB, ISBN 1-58023-016-4 **$16.95**

Putting God on the Guest List, 2nd Ed. AWARD WINNER!
How to Reclaim the Spiritual Meaning of Your Child's Bar or Bat Mitzvah
by Rabbi Jeffrey K. Salkin 6 x 9, 224 pp, Quality PB, ISBN 1-879045-59-1 **$16.95**

The Bar/Bat Mitzvah Memory Book: *An Album for Treasuring the Spiritual Celebration* by Rabbi Jeffrey K. Salkin and Nina Salkin
8 x 10, 48 pp, Deluxe HC, 2-color text, ribbon marker, ISBN 1-58023-111-X **$19.95**

For Kids—Putting God on Your Guest List
How to Claim the Spiritual Meaning of Your Bar or Bat Mitzvah
by Rabbi Jeffrey K. Salkin 6 x 9, 144 pp, Quality PB, ISBN 1-58023-015-6 **$14.95**

Bar/Bat Mitzvah Basics, 2nd Ed.: *A Practical Family Guide to Coming of Age Together*
Ed. by Cantor Helen Leneman 6 x 9, 240 pp, Quality PB, ISBN 1-58023-151-9 **$18.95**

Hanukkah, 2nd Ed.: *The Family Guide to Spiritual Celebration*—The Art of Jewish Living
by Dr. Ron Wolfson 7 x 9, 240 pp, Quality PB, Illus., ISBN 1-58023-122-5 **$18.95**

Shabbat, 2nd Ed.: *Preparing for and Celebrating the Sabbath*—The Art of Jewish Living
by Dr. Ron Wolfson 7 x 9, 320 pp, Quality PB, Illus., ISBN 1-58023-164-0 **$19.95**

The Passover Seder—The Art of Jewish Living
by Dr. Ron Wolfson 7 x 9, 352 pp, Quality PB, Illus., ISBN 1-879045-93-1 **$16.95**

Children's Spirituality

In Our Image
God's First Creatures   AWARD WINNER!
For ages 4 & up

by *Nancy Sohn Swartz*
Full-color illus. by *Melanie Hall*

A playful new twist on the Creation story—from the perspective of the animals. Celebrates the interconnectedness of nature and the harmony of all living things. "The vibrantly colored illustrations nearly leap off the page in this delightful interpretation." —*School Library Journal*
9 x 12, 32 pp, HC, Full-color illus., ISBN 1-879045-99-0 **$16.95**

God's Paintbrush   AWARD WINNER!
For ages 4 & up

by *Sandy Eisenberg Sasso*; Full-color illus. by *Annette Compton*

Invites children of all faiths and backgrounds to encounter God openly in their own lives. Wonderfully interactive; provides questions adult and child can explore together at the end of each episode. 11 x 8½, 32 pp, HC, Full-color illus., ISBN 1-879045-22-2 **$16.95**

Also available: A Teacher's Guide: **A Guide for Jewish & Christian Educators and Parents**
8½ x 11, 32 pp, PB, ISBN 1-879045-57-5 **$8.95**

God's Paintbrush Celebration Kit 9½ x 12, HC, Includes 5 sessions/40 full-color Activity Sheets and Teacher Folder with complete instructions, ISBN 1-58023-050-4 **$21.95**

In God's Name   AWARD WINNER!
For ages 4 & up

by *Sandy Eisenberg Sasso*; Full-color illus. by *Phoebe Stone*

Like an ancient myth in its poetic text and vibrant illustrations, this award-winning modern fable about the search for God's name celebrates the diversity and, at the same time, the unity of all people. 9 x 12, 32 pp, HC, Full-color illus., ISBN 1-879045-26-5 **$16.95**

What Is God's Name? (A Board Book)
For ages 0–4

An abridged board book version of award-winning *In God's Name.*
5 x 5, 24 pp, Board, Full-color illus., ISBN 1-893361-10-1 **$7.95** A SKYLIGHT PATHS Book

The 11th Commandment: *Wisdom from Our Children*
For all ages

by *The Children of America*   AWARD WINNER!

"If there were an Eleventh Commandment, what would it be?" Children of many religious denominations across America answer this question—in their own drawings and words. "A rare book of spiritual celebration for all people, of all ages, for all time."—*Bookviews*
8 x 10, 48 pp, HC, Full-color illus., ISBN 1-879045-46-X **$16.95**

Children's Spirituality

Because Nothing Looks Like God

by *Lawrence and Karen Kushner*

Full-color illus. by *Dawn W. Majewski*

For ages 4 & up

MULTICULTURAL, NONDENOMINATIONAL, NONSECTARIAN

What is God like? The first collaborative work by husband-and-wife team Lawrence and Karen Kushner introduces children to the possibilities of spiritual life. Real-life examples of happiness and sadness—from goodnight stories, to the hope and fear felt the first time at bat, to the closing moments of life—invite us to explore, together with our children, the questions we all have about God, no matter what our age.

11 x 8½, 32 pp, HC, Full-color illus., ISBN 1-58023-092-X **$16.95**

*Also available: **Teacher's Guide**, 8½ x 11, 22 pp, PB, ISBN 1-58023-140-3 **$6.95** For ages 5–8*

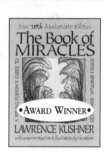

Where Is God?
What Does God Look Like?
How Does God Make Things Happen? (Board Books)

For ages 0–4

by *Lawrence and Karen Kushner*; Full-color illus. by *Dawn W. Majewski*

Gently invites children to become aware of God's presence all around them. Three board books abridged from *Because Nothing Looks Like God* by Lawrence and Karen Kushner.
Each 5 x 5, 24 pp, Board, Full-color illus. **$7.95** SKYLIGHT PATHS Books

Sharing Blessings
Children's Stories for Exploring the Spirit of the Jewish Holidays

For ages 6 & up

by *Rahel Musleah* and *Rabbi Michael Klayman*; Full-color illus.

What is the spiritual message of each of the Jewish holidays? How do we teach it to our children? Through stories about one family's life, *Sharing Blessings* explores ways to get into the *spirit* of thirteen different holidays.

8½ x 11, 64 pp, HC, Full-color illus., ISBN 1-879045-71-0 **$18.95**

The Book of Miracles   AWARD WINNER!
A Young Person's Guide to Jewish Spiritual Awareness

For ages 9 & up

by *Lawrence Kushner*

Introduces kids to a way of everyday spiritual thinking to last a lifetime. Kushner, whose award-winning books have brought spirituality to life for countless adults, now shows young people how to use Judaism as a foundation on which to build their lives.

6 x 9, 96 pp, HC, 2-color illus., ISBN 1-879045-78-8 **$16.95**

Spirituality

My People's Prayer Book: *Traditional Prayers, Modern Commentaries*
Ed. by *Dr. Lawrence A. Hoffman*

Provides a diverse and exciting commentary to the traditional liturgy, helping modern men and women find new wisdom in Jewish prayer, and bring liturgy into their lives. Each book includes Hebrew text, modern translation, and commentaries *from all perspectives* of the Jewish world.
Vol. 1—*The Sh'ma and Its Blessings,* 7 x 10, 168 pp, HC, ISBN 1-879045-79-6 **$23.95**
Vol. 2—*The Amidah,* 7 x 10, 240 pp, HC, ISBN 1-879045-80-X **$23.95**
Vol. 3—*P'sukei D'zimrah* (Morning Psalms), 7 x 10, 240 pp, HC, ISBN 1-879045-81-8 **$24.95**
Vol. 4—*Seder K'riat Hatorah* (The Torah Service), 7 x 10, 264 pp, HC, ISBN 1-879045-82-6 **$23.95**
Vol. 5—*Birkhot Hashachar* (Morning Blessings), 7 x 10, 240 pp, HC, ISBN 1-879045-83-4 **$24.95**
Vol. 6—*Tachanun and Concluding Prayers,* 7 x 10, 240 pp, HC, ISBN 1-879045-84-2 **$24.95**

Six Jewish Spiritual Paths: *A Rationalist Looks at Spirituality*
by Rabbi Rifat Sonsino
6 x 9, 208 pp, Quality PB, ISBN 1-58023-167-5 **$16.95**; HC, ISBN 1-58023-095-4 **$21.95**

Becoming a Congregation of Learners
Learning as a Key to Revitalizing Congregational Life by Isa Aron, Ph.D.;
Foreword by Rabbi Lawrence A. Hoffman, Co-Developer, Synagogue 2000
6 x 9, 304 pp, Quality PB, ISBN 1-58023-089-X **$19.95**

Self, Struggle & Change
Family Conflict Stories in Genesis and Their Healing Insights for Our Lives
by Dr. Norman J. Cohen 6 x 9, 224 pp, Quality PB, ISBN 1-879045-66-4 **$16.95**

Voices from Genesis: *Guiding Us through the Stages of Life*
by Dr. Norman J. Cohen 6 x 9, 192 pp, Quality PB, ISBN 1-58023-118-7 **$16.95**

Ancient Secrets: *Using the Stories of the Bible to Improve Our Everyday Lives*
by Rabbi Levi Meier, Ph.D. 5½ x 8½, 288 pp, Quality PB, ISBN 1-58023-064-4 **$16.95**

The Business Bible: *10 New Commandments for Bringing Spirituality &*
Ethical Values into the Workplace
by Rabbi Wayne Dosick 5½ x 8½, 208 pp, Quality PB, ISBN 1-58023-101-2 **$14.95**

Being God's Partner: *How to Find the Hidden Link Between Spirituality and Your Work*
by Rabbi Jeffrey K. Salkin; Intro. by Norman Lear AWARD WINNER!
6 x 9, 192 pp, Quality PB, ISBN 1-879045-65-6 **$16.95**; HC, ISBN 1-879045-37-0 **$19.95**

God & the Big Bang
Discovering Harmony Between Science & Spirituality AWARD WINNER!
by Daniel C. Matt 6 x 9, 224 pp, Quality PB, ISBN 1-879045-89-3 **$16.95**

Soul Judaism: *Dancing with God into a New Era*
by Rabbi Wayne Dosick 5½ x 8½, 304 pp, Quality PB, ISBN 1-58023-053-9 **$16.95**

Finding Joy: *A Practical Spiritual Guide to Happiness* AWARD WINNER!
by Rabbi Dannel I. Schwartz with Mark Hass
6 x 9, 192 pp, Quality PB, ISBN 1-58023-009-1 **$14.95**; HC, ISBN 1-879045-53-2 **$19.95**

Women's Spirituality

The Women's Torah Commentary: *New Insights from Women Rabbis on the 54 Weekly Torah Portions* Ed. by *Rabbi Elyse Goldstein*

For the first time, women rabbis provide a commentary on the entire Five Books of Moses. More than twenty-five years after the first woman was ordained a rabbi in America, these inspiring teachers bring their rich perspectives to bear on the biblical text. In a week-by-week format; a perfect gift for others, or for yourself. 6 x 9, 496 pp, HC, ISBN 1-58023-076-8 **$34.95**

Moonbeams: *A Hadassah Rosh Hodesh Guide*
Ed. by *Carol Diament, Ph.D.*

This hands-on "idea book" focuses on *Rosh Hodesh*, the festival of the new moon, as a source of spiritual growth for Jewish women. A complete sourcebook that will initiate or rejuvenate women's study groups, it is also perfect for women preparing for *bat mitzvah*, or for anyone interested in learning more about *Rosh Hodesh* observance and what it has to offer. 8½ x 11, 240 pp, Quality PB, ISBN 1-58023-099-7 **$20.00**

Lifecycles In Two Volumes **AWARD WINNERS!**
V. 1: *Jewish Women on Life Passages & Personal Milestones*
Ed. and with Intros. by Rabbi Debra Orenstein
V. 2: *Jewish Women on Biblical Themes in Contemporary Life*
Ed. and with Intros. by Rabbi Debra Orenstein and Rabbi Jane Rachel Litman
V. 1: 6 x 9, 480 pp, Quality PB, ISBN 1-58023-018-0 **$19.95**
V. 2: 6 x 9, 464 pp, Quality PB, ISBN 1-58023-019-9 **$19.95**

ReVisions: *Seeing Torah through a Feminist Lens* **AWARD WINNER!**
by Rabbi Elyse Goldstein 5½ x 8½, 224 pp, Quality PB, ISBN 1-58023-117-9 **$16.95**;
208 pp, HC, ISBN 1-58023-047-4 **$19.95**

The Year Mom Got Religion: *One Woman's Midlife Journey into Judaism*
by Lee Meyerhoff Hendler 6 x 9, 208 pp, Quality PB, ISBN 1-58023-070-9 **$15.95**

Ecology

Torah of the Earth: *Exploring 4,000 Years of Ecology in Jewish Thought*
In 2 Volumes Ed. by *Rabbi Arthur Waskow*

An invaluable key to understanding the intersection of ecology and Judaism. Leading scholars provide a guided tour of Jewish ecological thought.
Vol. 1: *Biblical Israel & Rabbinic Judaism*, 6 x 9, 272 pp, Quality PB, ISBN 1-58023-086-5 **$19.95**
Vol. 2: *Zionism & Eco-Judaism*, 6 x 9, 336 pp, Quality PB, ISBN 1-58023-087-3 **$19.95**

Ecology & the Jewish Spirit: *Where Nature & the Sacred Meet* Ed. and with Intros.
by Ellen Bernstein 6 x 9, 288 pp, Quality PB, ISBN 1-58023-082-2 **$16.95**

The Jewish Gardening Cookbook: *Growing Plants & Cooking for Holidays & Festivals*
by Michael Brown 6 x 9, 224 pp, Illus., Quality PB, ISBN 1-58023-116-0 **$16.95**;
HC, ISBN 1-58023-004-0 **$21.95**

Spirituality—The Kushner Series
Books by Lawrence Kushner

The Way Into Jewish Mystical Tradition
Explains the principles of Jewish mystical thinking, their religious and spiritual significance, and how they relate to our lives. A book that allows us to experience and understand the Jewish mystical approach to our place in the world.
6 x 9, 224 pp, HC, ISBN 1-58023-029-6 **$21.95**

Jewish Spirituality: *A Brief Introduction for Christians*
Addresses Christian's questions, revealing the essence of Judaism in a way that people whose own tradition traces its roots to Judaism can understand and appreciate.
5½ x 8½, 112 pp, Quality PB, ISBN 1-58023-150-0 **$12.95**

Eyes Remade for Wonder: *The Way of Jewish Mysticism and Sacred Living*
A Lawrence Kushner Reader Intro. by *Thomas Moore*

Whether you are new to Kushner or a devoted fan, you'll find inspiration here. With samplings from each of Kushner's works, and a generous amount of new material, this book is to be read and reread, each time discovering deeper layers of meaning in our lives.
6 x 9, 240 pp, Quality PB, ISBN 1-58023-042-3 **$18.95**; HC, ISBN 1-58023-014-8 **$23.95**

   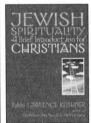 

Invisible Lines of Connection: *Sacred Stories of the Ordinary* AWARD WINNER!
5½ x 8½, 160 pp, Quality PB, ISBN 1-879045-98-2 **$15.95**

Honey from the Rock: *An Introduction to Jewish Mysticism* SPECIAL ANNIVERSARY EDITION
6 x 9, 176 pp, Quality PB, ISBN 1-58023-073-3 **$15.95**

The Book of Letters: *A Mystical Hebrew Alphabet* AWARD WINNER!
Popular HC Edition, 6 x 9, 80 pp, 2-color text, ISBN 1-879045-00-1 **$24.95**; *Deluxe Gift Edition*, 9 x 12, 80 pp, HC, 4-color text, ornamentation, slipcase, ISBN 1-879045-01-X **$79.95**; *Collector's Limited Edition*, 9 x 12, 80 pp, HC, gold-embossed pages, hand-assembled slipcase. With silkscreened print. Limited to 500 signed and numbered copies, ISBN 1-879045-04-4 **$349.00**

The Book of Words: *Talking Spiritual Life, Living Spiritual Talk* AWARD WINNER!
6 x 9, 160 pp, Quality PB, 2-color text, ISBN 1-58023-020-2 **$16.95**; HC, ISBN 1-879045-35-4 **$21.95**

God Was in This Place & I, i Did Not Know: *Finding Self, Spirituality and Ultimate Meaning*
6 x 9, 192 pp, Quality PB, ISBN 1-879045-33-8 **$16.95**

The River of Light: *Jewish Mystical Awareness* SPECIAL ANNIVERSARY EDITION
6 x 9, 192 pp, Quality PB, ISBN 1-58023-096-2 **$16.95**

Because Nothing Looks Like God
by Lawrence and Karen Kushner; Full-color illus. by Dawn W. Majewski
11 x 8½, 32 pp, HC, Full-color illus., ISBN 1-58023-092-X **$16.95** For ages 4 & up

Spirituality & More

The Jewish Lights Spirituality Handbook
A Guide to Understanding, Exploring & Living a Spiritual Life
Ed. by *Stuart M. Matlins, Editor in Chief, Jewish Lights Publishing*

Rich, creative material from over fifty spiritual leaders on every aspect of Jewish spirituality today: prayer, meditation, mysticism, study, rituals, special days, the everyday, and more.
6 x 9, 456 pp, Quality PB, ISBN 1-58023-093-8 **$18.95**; HC, ISBN 1-58023-100-4 **$24.95**

The Story of the Jews: *A 4,000-Year Adventure—A Graphic History Book*
Written and illustrated by *Stan Mack*

Through witty cartoons and accurate narrative, illustrates the major characters and events that have shaped the Jewish people and culture. For all ages.
6 x 9, 304 pp, Quality PB, Illus., ISBN 1-58023-155-1 **$16.95**

The Jewish Prophet: *Visionary Words from Moses and Miriam to Henrietta Szold and A. J. Heschel*
by *Rabbi Dr. Michael J. Shire*

This beautifully illustrated collection of Jewish prophecy features the lives and teachings of thirty men and women, from biblical times to modern day. Provides an inspiring and informative description of the role each played in their own time, and an explanation of why we should know about them in our time. Illustrated with illuminations from medieval Hebrew manuscripts.
6½ x 8½, 128 pp, HC, 123 full-color illus., ISBN 1-58023-168-3 **$25.00**

The Enneagram and Kabbalah: *Reading Your Soul*
by Rabbi Howard A. Addison 6 x 9, 176 pp, Quality PB, ISBN 1-58023-001-6 **$15.95**

Cast in God's Image: *Discover Your Personality Type Using the Enneagram and Kabbalah*
by Rabbi Howard A. Addison 7 x 9, 176 pp, Quality PB, ISBN 1-58023-124-1 **$16.95**

Mystery Midrash: *An Anthology of Jewish Mystery & Detective Fiction* AWARD WINNER!
Ed. by Lawrence W. Raphael 6 x 9, 304 pp, Quality PB, ISBN 1-58023-055-5 **$16.95**

Criminal Kabbalah: *An Intriguing Anthology of Jewish Mystery & Detective Fiction*
Ed. by Lawrence W. Raphael; Foreword by Laurie R. King
6 x 9, 256 pp, Quality PB, ISBN 1-58023-109-8 **$16.95**

Sacred Intentions: *Daily Inspiration to Strengthen the Spirit, Based on Jewish Wisdom*
by Rabbi Kerry M. Olitzky & Rabbi Lori Forman
4½ x 6½, 448 pp, Quality PB, ISBN 1-58023-061-X **$15.95**

Restful Reflections: *Nighttime Inspiration to Calm the Soul, Based on Jewish Wisdom*
by Rabbi Kerry M. Olitzky & Rabbi Lori Forman
4½ x 6½, 448 pp, Quality PB, ISBN 1-58023-091-1 **$15.95**

Embracing the Covenant: *Converts to Judaism Talk About Why & How* Ed. by Rabbi Allan Berkowitz & Patti Moskovitz 6 x 9, 192 pp, Quality PB, ISBN 1-879045-50-8 **$16.95**

Wandering Stars: *An Anthology of Jewish Fantasy & Science Fiction* Ed. by Jack Dann; Intro. by Isaac Asimov 6 x 9, 272 pp, Quality PB, ISBN 1-58023-005-9 **$16.95**

Israel—A Spiritual Travel Guide: *A Companion for the Modern Jewish Pilgrim* AWARD WINNER!
by Rabbi Lawrence A. Hoffman 4¾ x 10, 256 pp, Quality PB, ISBN 1-879045-56-7 **$18.95**

Spirituality

The Dance of the Dolphin
Finding Prayer, Perspective and Meaning in the Stories of Our Lives
by *Karyn D. Kedar*

Helps you decode the three "languages" we all must learn—prayer, perspective, meaning—to weave the seemingly ordinary and extraordinary together.
6 x 9, 176 pp, HC, ISBN 1-58023-154-3 **$19.95**

Does the Soul Survive?
A Jewish Journey to Belief in Afterlife, Past Lives & Living with Purpose
by *Rabbi Elie Kaplan Spitz*; Foreword by *Brian L. Weiss, M.D.*

Spitz relates his own experiences and those shared with him by people he has worked with as a rabbi, and shows us that belief in afterlife and past lives, so often approached with reluctance, is in fact true to Jewish tradition.
6 x 9, 288 pp, Quality PB, ISBN 1-58023-165-9 **$16.95**; HC, ISBN 1-58023-094-6 **$21.95**

The Gift of Kabbalah
Discovering the Secrets of Heaven, Renewing Your Life on Earth
by *Tamar Frankiel, Ph.D.*

Makes accessible the mysteries of Kabbalah. Traces Kabbalah's evolution in Judaism and shows us its most important gift: a way of revealing the connection between our "everyday" life and the spiritual oneness of the universe. 6 x 9, 256 pp, HC, ISBN 1-58023-108-X **$21.95**

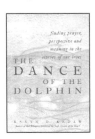 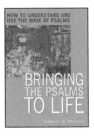   

God Whispers: *Stories of the Soul, Lessons of the Heart*
by Karyn D. Kedar 6 x 9, 176 pp, Quality PB, ISBN 1-58023-088-1 **$15.95**

Bringing the Psalms to Life: *How to Understand and Use the Book of Psalms*
by Rabbi Daniel F. Polish
6 x 9, 208 pp, Quality PB, ISBN 1-58023-157-8 **$16.95**; HC, ISBN 1-58023-077-6 **$21.95**

The Empty Chair: *Finding Hope and Joy—*
Timeless Wisdom from a Hasidic Master, Rebbe Nachman of Breslov AWARD WINNER!
4 x 6, 128 pp, Deluxe PB, 2-color text, ISBN 1-879045-67-2 **$9.95**

The Gentle Weapon: *Prayers for Everyday and Not-So-Everyday Moments*
Adapted from the Wisdom of Rebbe Nachman of Breslov
4 x 6, 144 pp, Deluxe PB, 2-color text, ISBN 1-58023-022-9 **$9.95**

Or phone, fax, mail or e-mail to: JEWISH LIGHTS Publishing
Sunset Farm Offices, Route 4 • P.O. Box 237 • Woodstock, Vermont 05091
Tel: (802) 457-4000 • Fax: (802) 457-4004 • www.jewishlights.com
Credit card orders: (800) 962-4544 (8:30AM–5:30PM ET Monday–Friday)
Generous discounts on quantity orders. SATISFACTION GUARANTEED. Prices subject to change.